CW00496503

A Paines Plough, Soho Theatre
and Sheffield Theatres production

RUN SISTER RUN

Chloë Moss

Supported by
**ARTS COUNCIL
ENGLAND**

Run Sister Run
by Chloë Moss

CAST

CONNIE	Lucy Ellinson
URSULA	Helena Lymbery
ADRIAN	Silas Carson
JACK	Lucas Button

PRODUCTION TEAM

Director	Charlotte Bennett
Designer	Rosie Elnile
Lighting Designer	Zoe Spurr
Composer & Sound Designer	Arun Ghosh
Movement Director	Laura Cubitt
Fight Director	Alison De Burgh
Casting Director	Nadine Rennie CDG
Accent Coach	Elspeth Morrison
Dramaturg	Sarah Dickenson
Assistant Director	Matilda Ibini
Assistant Director	Lucy Grace McCann
Production Manager	Stephanie Balmforth
Stage Manager	Rachael Head
Deputy Stage Manager	Robyn Clogg
Assistant Stage Manager	Robert Perkins
Costume Supervisor	Jackie Orton

CAST AND CREATIVE TEAM

CHLOË MOSS (Writer)

Chloë is an accomplished playwright and screenwriter. Her celebrated play THIS WIDE NIGHT 2008/2009 (Clean Break/Soho) won the prestigious Susan Smith Blackburn Prize and was subsequently produced Off-Broadway. Chloë has written numerous other shows including THE GATEKEEPER 2012 (Royal Exchange Theatre); FATAL LIGHT 2010/2011 (Soho); CHRISTMAS IS MILES AWAY 2005/2006 (Bush/Off-Broadway); and HOW LOVE IS SPELT 2002 (Bush/New York's Summer Play Festival).

She is currently under commission to the Royal Court and Headlong Theatre.

Chloë has also written extensively for television. She is currently developing original TV projects and is working on an original teen drama for CBBC. She is also under commission to BBC Radio 4.

LUCY ELLINSON (Connie)

Theatre credits include: MACBETH (Royal Exchange Theatre); TOP GIRLS (National Theatre); JUBILEE (Lyric Hammersmith/Royal Exchange Theatre); KINGDOM COME, A MIDSUMMER NIGHT'S DREAM: PLAY FOR THE NATION (RSC); THE RESISTABLE RISE OF ARTURO UI (Donmar Warehouse); GROUNDED, THE CHRISTIANS, TROJAN WOMEN, TENET (Gate Theatre); WORLD FACTORY (Metis Arts/Young Vic/New Wolsey); MAD MAN (Chris Goode/Theatre Royal Plymouth).

Television includes: BRITANNIA, NEW TRICKS.

HELENA LYMBERY (Ursula)

Theatre credits include: MR GUM AND THE DANCING BEAR, TREASURE ISLAND, THIS HOUSE, THE CAT IN THE HAT, ...SOME TRACE OF HER, WOMEN OF TROY, ATTEMPTS ON HER LIFE, IPHIGENIA AT AULIS, HIS DARK MATERIALS, WICKED YAAR, HENRY V (National Theatre); DEAR ELIZABETH (Gate Theatre); QUEEN MARGARET (Royal Exchange Theatre); PITY (Royal Court); WOLVES ARE COMING FOR YOU (Pentabus); HARRY POTTER AND THE CURSED CHILD (West End); WE WANT YOU TO WATCH (RashDash/National Theatre); THE SECRET AGENT (Young Vic/Theatre O); AFTER DIDO (Young Vic/ENO); SLEEPING BEAUTY(Young Vic); COASTING (Bristol Old Vic).

Television includes: DOCTOR FOSTER; FATHER BROWN; OLIVER TWIST; ALASTAIR MCGOWAN'S BIG IMPRESSION; THE INSPECTOR LYNLEY MYSTERIES.

Film includes: LONDON ROAD.

SILAS CARSON (Adrian)

Recent theatre credits include: THE CAPTIVE QUEEN (Shakespeare's Globe); OCCUPATIONAL HAZARD, DRAWING THE LINE (Hampstead Theatre); HALF LIFE (Theatre Royal Bath); A MIDSUMMER NIGHT'S DREAM (Royal & Derngate Northampton); THE PROPHET (Gate Theatre); THE COMEDY OF ERRORS (National Theatre); RUINED, MACBETH (Almeida Theatre); ARABIAN NIGHTS (RSC); MUCH ADO ABOUT NOTHING (Regent's Park Open Air Theatre).

Recent film credits include: THE CORRUPTED, POSTCARDS FROM LONDON, MISS YOU ALREADY.

Recent television credits include: THE ACCIDENT, SICK OF IT, SILENT WITNESS, TRUST, EASTENDERS, UNFORGOTTEN, INDIAN SUMMERS, THE CASUAL VACANCY, THE 'C' WORD, GLUE.

LUCAS BUTTON (Jack)

Theatre credits include: WAR HORSE (National Theatre/UK tour); THE BUTTERFLY LION (Chichester Festival Theatre); KES (Leeds Playhouse); ALAN, WE THINK YOU SHOULD GET A DOG (New Diorama Theatre); THE WINTER'S TALE (English National Opera); PINOCCHIO, A TENDER THING (The Dukes Theatre); THE LOST PALACE (Fuel Theatre & Uninvited Guests). His short film credits include BILLY AND JAKE (Andrew Jonathan Smith).

CHARLOTTE BENNETT (Director)

Charlotte is Joint Artistic Director of Paines Plough. Previously she was Associate Director at Soho Theatre where she led the new writing department. Credits for Soho Theatre include: WHITEWASH by Gabriel Bisset-Smith, HAPPY HOUR by Jack Rooke and Waltham Forest Parks Festival. Prior to this she was Artistic Director of Forward Theatre Project; an artists' collective she founded. For Forward Theatre Project she made and directed new plays that toured nationally, inspired by working in partnership with different communities around the UK at venues including: National Theatre; York Theatre Royal; Northern Stage; Derby Theatre; Live Theatre and The Lowry. As a freelance director, she has worked extensively for Open Clasp Theatre Company, creating new plays inspired by marginalised women in the north-east. She also held the role of Producer for theatre company RashDash where she toured experimental new theatre around the UK.

ROSIE ELNILE (Designer)

Theatre includes: [BLANK] (Donmar Warehouse); OUR TOWN (Regent's Park Open Air Theatre); THE RIDICULOUS DARKNESS, UNKNOWN ISLAND, THE CONVERT (Gate Theatre); THE AMERICAN CLOCK (Old Vic); THE WOLVES (Theatre Royal Stratford East); THE MYSTERIES, THREE SISTERS (Royal Exchange, Manchester); ABANDON (Lyric Hammersmith); RETURNING TO HAIFA (Finborough Theatre); GOATS (Royal Court); PRIME TIME (Royal Court Schools Tour); BIG GUNS (The Yard).

ZOE SPURR (Lighting Designer)

Zoe trained at Royal Central School of Speech and Drama.

Recent theatre includes: WUTHERING HEIGHTS (Royal Exchange); AN EDINBURGH CHRISTMAS CAROL (Lyceum Edinburgh); A MIDSUMMER NIGHT'S DREAM (National Youth Theatre/Criterion Theatre); THE SEVEN AGES OF PATIENCE (Kiln Theatre); HEDDA TESMAN (Headlong/Chichester Festival Theatre); ONEGIN, GEORGIANA, and LUCIO PAPIRIO DITTATORE for Buxton International Festival (Buxton Opera House); A MAN WITHOUT A PAST (New Perspectives/UK tour); EMILIA (Vaudeville Theatre); THE PHLEBOTOMIST (Hampstead Theatre); THE MAIDS (HOME, Manchester); CAT IN THE HAT (Leicester Curve/UK tour); THE UNRETURNING (Frantic Assembly/UK tour); SILENCE (Mercury Theatre/UK tour); TOAST (The Other Palace/Traverse 1); MEEK (Headlong/UK tour); ABIGAIL'S PARTY; ABI (Queen's Theatre Hornchurch/UK tour); POLSTEAD (Eastern Angles/UK tour); STICKY, INFINITE JOY, CONFIDENCE, NATIVES, COLLECTIVE RAGE (Southwark Playhouse); TINY DYNAMITE (Old Red Lion); NOT TALKING (Arcola); GROTTY (Bunker); PHOENIX RISING, LOOSE LIPS (Big House Theatre Company, Site Specific); THE BEGINNERS (Unicorn Theatre); ELEPHANT (Birmingham REP); THE MAGIC FLUTE (Soho Theatre/UK tour).

For portfolio, please see zoespurrlighting.co.uk

ARUN GHOSH (Composer & Sound Designer)

Arun Ghosh is a British-Asian musician and composer.

Twice awarded 'Jazz Instrumentalist of the Year' at the Parliamentary Jazz Awards, Ghosh leads his own ensembles, touring nationally and internationally. He has released four albums on camoci records: NORTHERN NAMASTE, PRIMAL ODYSSEY, A SOUTH ASIAN SUITE, and BUT WHERE ARE YOU REALLY FROM?

As a composer for theatre, Ghosh has contributed scores and sound design to a wide array of productions since his debut in 2002; STORM by Lemn Sissay at Contact, Manchester.

Recent theatre composition includes: THE WOLF, THE DUCK AND THE MOUSE (Unicorn/New Perspectives); A DOLL'S HOUSE (Lyric Hammersmith); BYSTANDERS (Cardboard Citizens); HOBSON'S CHOICE (Royal Exchange, Manchester); NOUGHTS & CROSSES (Pilot Theatre/Derby Theatre); APPROACHING EMPTY (Tamasha/Kiln Theatre); MUCH ADO ABOUT NOTHING (Watford Palace Theatre); LIONS AND TIGERS (Shakespeare's Globe Theatre).

Arun Ghosh is a Creative Associate at Watford Palace Theatre, and an Associate Artist of Z-arts, Manchester.

LAURA CUBITT (Movement Director)

Laura is a Movement & Puppetry Director and Performer.

Theatre includes, as Movement Director: ANNA (National Theatre, Associate Movement Director); OPPENHEIMER (West End); WARHORSE (Associate Movement Director, National Theatre, Berlin); 2012 Olympics Opening (Associate Movement Director).

As Puppetry Director: THE BOY IN THE DRESS (RSC); DON QUIXOTE (RSC, Puppetry Co-director); A

MONSTER CALLS (The Old Vic/Bristol Old Vic/Chichester Festival Theatre); SMALL ISLAND, COMMON (National Theatre); DINOSAUR WORLD LIVE (UK & US tour); RUDOLPH (Birmingham Mac); THE CURIOUS INCIDENT OF THE DOG IN THE NIGHT TIME (National Theatre/West End, Puppetry Consultant); BRILLIANT (Fevered Sleep, Puppetry Consultant); RUNNING WILD (Chichester Festival Theatre/UK tour, Associate Puppetry Director); GOODNIGHT MR TOM (West End/UK tour, Associate Puppetry Director).

As a Performer: PETER PAN, ELEPHANTOM, WOMEN BEWARE WOMEN (National Theatre); WAR HORSE (National Theatre/West End); THE LORAX (The Old Vic); RUNNING WILD (Regent's Park Open Air Theatre); GOODNIGHT MR TOM (Chichester Festival Theatre); FAERIES (Royal Opera House).

ALISON DE BURGH (Fight Director)

Theatre credits include: THE MAN IN THE WHITE SUIT (West End); MY COUSIN RACHEL, WHAT'S IN A NAME?, THE GIRL ON THE TRAIN (UK tour); ROMEO AND JULIET (Shakespeare's Globe); THE LAST KING OF SCOTLAND (Sheffield Crucible); JUBILEE (Manchester Royal Exchange); THE LADYKILLERS (Lyric Belfast); ELEPHANT (Birmingham Rep); INTEMPERANCE (New Vic); THE SWEET SCIENCE OF BRUISING (Southwark Playhouse); A VIEW FROM THE BRIDGE, THE SCOTSBORO BOYS (Young Vic); A SMALL FAMILY BUSINESS (National Theatre); IT'S A MAD WORLD MY MASTERS (RSC).

Opera credits include: OKLAHOMA! (Grange Park Opera); JOSEPH AND HIS AMAZING TECHNICOLOUR DREAMCOAT (Killworth House); CAROUSEL (Opera North); DON GIOVANNI (Glyndebourne Festival Opera); FLORENTINE TRAGEDY; GIANNI SCHICCI (Greek National Opera); VARJAK PAW (The Opera Group); THE TROJANS AT CARTHAGE (English National Opera).

Film credits include: MINDHORN, THE WALL OF LYON, BEING OTHELLO, MINE, THE DARK ROOM, GHOST STORY, STUBBORN AND SPITE, FOUR, RESPECT, PROMISES, PROMISES.

Television credits include: LEMON LA VIDA LOCA, MAESTRO, THE HOUR, THE ELEVENTH HOUR.

Alison was the first ever female to become an Equity-registered Fight Director.

NADINE RENNIE CDG (Casting Director)

Nadine was in-house Casting Director at Soho Theatre for fifteen years; working on new plays by writers including Dennis Kelly, Bryony Lavery, Arinzé Kene, Roy Williams, Philip Ridley, Laura Wade and Vicky Jones.

Since going freelance in January 2019 Nadine's credits include: THE GLASS MENAGERIE, HOARD (Arcola); GOOD DOG (tiata fahodzi); LITTLE BABY JESUS (Orange Tree Theatre); THE LAST KING OF SCOTLAND (Sheffield Crucible); RANDOM, THERE ARE NO BEGINNINGS (Leeds Playhouse); THE LITTLE PRINCE (Fuel Theatre); PRICE (National Theatre of Wales) and Nadine continues to cast for Soho Theatre – most recently WHITEWASH, TYPICAL, SHUCK 'N' JIVE and THE SPECIAL RELATIONSHIP.

Television work includes: BAFTA-winning CBBC series Dixi, casting the first three series.

Nadine also has a long-running association as Casting Director for Synergy Theatre Project and is a member of the Casting Directors Guild.

ELSPETH MORRISON (Accent Coach)

Theatre credits include: DIAL M FOR MURDER (Richmond Theatre); THE CROFT (Original Theatre); AMELIE (The Other Palace); MY COUSIN RACHEL (Theatre Royal Bath); HOW THE GRINCH STOLE CHRISTMAS (UK tour); ROUNDABOUT Plays, I WANNA BE YOURS (Paines Plough); LITTLE VOICE (Theatre by the Lake); INK (Almeida); BASKERVILLE (Chinese tour); STRANGERS ON A TRAIN (UK tour); JERUSALEM (Watermill); SKELLIG (Nottingham Playhouse); WOLF OF WALL STREET (Sun Street); NAPOLI BROOKLYN (Park Theatre); HOGARTH'S SUCCESS (Rose Theatre); SKETCHING (Wilton's Music Hall); CONTRACTIONS (Deafinitely Theatre); TROUBLE IN MIND (Print Room); MY MOTHER SAID (Sheffield Crucible); INTEMPERANCE (New Vic).

Television credits include: HORRIBLE HISTORIES, PRIME SUSPECT 1973, CLIQUE, CORONATION STREET, EASTENDERS, ERIC, ERNIE AND ME, THE LOUDEST VOICE, DAS BOOT, FLATMATES, EASTENDERS, PICNIC AT HANGING ROCK.

Radio credits include: X FILES: COLDCASES, MY NAME IS WHY, THE TESTAMENTS.

Film credits include: THE MAD AXEMAN, WATCHER IN THE WOODS, THE PROFESSOR AND THE MADMAN, THE MORE YOU IGNORE ME.

Elspeth regularly makes expert contributions on programmes such as Melvyn Bragg's MATTER OF THE NORTH (BBC); AN IMMIGRANT'S GUIDE TO BRITAIN (Channel 4) and THE ROYALS (Netflix).

SARAH DICKENSON (Dramaturg)

Sarah is a freelance dramaturg and associate dramaturg for LAMDA and Paines Plough. Her roles have included: Associate Dramaturg for the RSC, Production Dramaturg for the Globe, Senior Reader at Soho Theatre, Literary Manager for Theatre503, New Writing Associate at The Red Room and founder of the South West New Writing Network.

She has worked on performance projects and artist development nationally and internationally for a wide range of organisations and theatre makers including: Nuffield

Theatre Southampton, Theatre Centre, National Theatre, Bristol Old Vic, Theatre Bristol, Old Vic New Voices, Liverpool Everyman, Champloo, Theatre Royal Bath, Plymouth Theatre Royal, Tamasha, Apples and Snakes, Almeida Theatre, Hall for Cornwall, The Fence and Churchill Theatre.

MATILDA IBINI (Assistant Director)

Matilda Ibini is an award-winning playwright, screenwriter (and occasional dramaturg) from London. She was awarded a scholarship from BAFTA and Warner Brothers to study a Masters in Playwriting & Screenwriting. She was part of the Royal Court Writers Program and was a member of Soho Theatre's Writers' Alumni Group. She has had residencies at Soho Theatre, BBC Writersroom, Graeae Theatre and the National Theatre Studio. Her play MUSCOVADO was produced by BurntOut Theatre and toured the UK in 2015.

MUSCOVADO subsequently co-won the Alfred Fagon Audience Award. Her radio play THE GRAPE THAT ROLLED UNDER THE FRIDGE was broadcast on BBC Radio 3. Her Offie-nominated play LITTLE MISS BURDEN premiered at the Bunker Theatre in 2019. Her work has been staged at the Old Vic Theatre, Shakespeare's Globe, Bush Theatre, Hampstead Theatre Downstairs, National Theatre Shed, St. James Theatre, Royal Exchange Manchester, Birmingham REP, Soho Theatre, Arcola Theatre, Bunker Theatre, Hackney Showroom and VAULT Festival.

LUCY GRACE MCCANN (Assistant Director)

Lucy Grace McCann is a theatre director from London. She is currently part of the Resident Director pool at the Almeida Theatre. Directing Credits include KARAOKE PLAY by Annie Jenkins (Bunker Theatre, 2019) and A TINDER TRILOGY by Annie Jenkins (Theatre503, 2019, and Hens

and Chickens Theatre, 2018). Lucy was previously Director in Residence at the Oxford Playhouse, Magdalen College School and Surbiton High School. Lucy holds an MA (Distinction) in Shakespeare and the British Tradition and a First Class BA (Hons) in English and Theatre Studies from the University of Warwick.

RACHAEL HEAD (Stage Manager)

Rachael is a Stage Manager with a background in Production. Her Stage Management credits include: TAMING OF THE SHREW (The Globe Theatre); WHITEWASH (Soho); SQUARE GO (Francesca Moody Productions); THE ARTIST (Circo Aereo); EUGENE ONEGIN (Opera Up Close); THE TALES OF KIERAN HODGSON (Berk's Nest); DICK WHITTINGTON (LP Creatives); DARE TO DO (Ka Zimba Theatre). Rachael has a BA (Hons) in Literature and started her own company, Stones Theatre in 2015 where she produced ELEGIES FOR ANGELS, PUNKS AND RAGING QUEENS (Bill Russell); CLOSER (Patrick Marber) and RADIANT VERMIN (Phillip Ridley) at the Modern Art Gallery, Oxford and The Bread and Roses Theatre, Clapham. Other Producer credits include: SCALPED (Initiative. dkf); cover on BABY REINDEER & DO OUR BEST (Francesca Moody Productions); In-House Producer at CentrE17; MODEL BEHAVIOUR (The Pleasance Theatre); THE S-WORD (Mind Mental Health) and 1st Assistant Director on NEW YOU, a feature film by Neilson Black.

ROBYN CLOGG (Deputy Stage Manager)

Robyn trained at Central School of Speech and Drama with a BA (Hons) in Theatre Practice, specialising in Stage Management.

Credits as Company Stage Manager include: REASONS TO STAY ALIVE (ETT/Sheffield Theatres); DISHOOM! (Rifco Theatre/Watford Palace

Theatre); THE WEIR (ETT/Mercury Theatre, Colchester); CITY OF GLASS (59 Productions/HOME Manchester/ Lyric Hammersmith).

Credits as Company Stage Manager (on the book) include: FASCINATING AIDA (Password Productions/UK tour); DILLIE KEANE (Password Productions/UK tour); THE TEMPEST (Watford Palace Theatre); I BELIEVE IN UNICORNS (Wizard Productions); DRAW ME A BIRD (Peut-être Theatre); MORECAMBE THE PLAY (UK tour/ Duchess Theatre).

As Deputy Stage Manager credits include: A MIDSUMMER NIGHT'S DREAM, OLIVER TWIST, PRIDE & PREJUDICE, LORD OF THE FLIES, TO KILL A MOCKINGBIRD (Regent's Park Open Air Theatre); THE WEIR (ETT/Mercury Theatre, Colchester); BRIDESHEAD REVISITED (ETT/York Theatre Royal); SHINE (Live Theatre Newcastle); TELL ME THE TRUTH ABOUT LOVE (Streetwise Opera); THE LIGHTHOUSE & IN THE LOCKED ROOM (Royal College of Music).

ROBERT PERKINS (Assistant Stage Manager)

Robert trained at LAMDA.

Recent work includes: THE OCEAN AT THE END OF THE LANE, ANNA, FOLLIES, NETWORK (National Theatre); MALORY TOWERS (Wise Children, UK tour); OTHELLO (Great Theatre of China, Shanghai).

PAINES PLOUGH

Paines Plough tours the best new theatre to all four corners of the UK and around the world. Whether you're in Liverpool or Lyme Regis, Brighton or Berwick-Upon-Tweed, a Paines Plough show is coming to a theatre near you soon.

'The lifeblood of the UK's theatre ecosystem.' *Guardian*

Paines Plough was formed in 1974 over a pint of Paines Bitter in the Plough pub. Since then we've produced more than 150 new productions by world renowned playwrights like Stephen Jeffreys, Abi Morgan, Sarah Kane, Mark Ravenhill, Dennis Kelly, Mike Bartlett, Kate Tempest and Vinay Patel. We've toured those plays to hundreds of places from Bristol to Belfast to Brisbane.

'That noble company Paines Plough, de facto national theatre of new writing.' *Daily Telegraph*

We tour to more than 30,000 people a year from Cornwall to the Orkney Islands; in village halls and Off-Broadway, at music festivals and student unions, online and on radio, and in our own pop-up theatre ROUNDABOUT.

Our 2020 Programme premieres the best new British plays touring the length and breadth of the UK in theatres, clubs and pubs everywhere from city centres to seaside towns. ROUNDABOUT hosts a jam-packed Edinburgh Festival Fringe programme and brings mini-festivals to each stop on its nationwide tour. Our COME TO WHERE I'M FROM app features short audio plays available to download free from the App Store and GooglePlay.

'I think some theatre just saved my life.' *@kate_clement on Twitter*

Soho Theatre is London's most vibrant theatre for new theatre, comedy and cabaret. They are a charity and social enterprise, driven by a passion for the work they produce, the artists they work with and the audiences they attract. Soho Theatre's home is in the heart of the West End – three performance spaces, a busy bar, and a fast-changing festival programme with up to six shows a night. Firmly established on the London cultural scene, they're now expanding into an additional 1,000 seat venue in Walthamstow, touring across the UK, India and Australia, and creating digital content.

We work with artists in a variety of ways, from full producing of new plays, to co-producing new work, working with associate artists and presenting the best new emerging theatre companies that we can find.

We have numerous artists on attachment and under commission, including Soho Six and a thriving Company of writers and comedy groups. We read and see hundreds of scripts and shows a year.

'The place was buzzing, and there were queues all over the building as audiences waited to go into one or other of the venue's spaces… exuberant and clearly anticipating a good time.' *Guardian*

We attract over 240,000 audience members a year at Soho Theatre, at festivals and through our national and international touring. We produced, co-produced or staged over 40 new plays in the last 12 months.

As an entrepreneurial charity and social enterprise, we have created an innovative and sustainable business model. We maximise value from Arts Council England and philanthropic funding, contributing more to government in tax and NI than we receive in public funding.

sohotheatre.com
@sohotheatre all social media

Registered Charity No: 267234

Soho Theatre, 21 Dean Street
London W1D 3NE
Admin 020 7287 5060
Box Office 020 7478 0100

OPPORTUNITIES FOR WRITERS
AT SOHO THEATRE

We are looking for unique and unheard voices – from all backgrounds, attitudes and places.

We want to make things you've never seen before.

Alongside workshops, readings and notes sessions, there are several ways writers can connect with Soho Theatre. You can

Enter our prestigious biennial competition the Verity Bargate Award just as Vicky Jones did in 2013 with her award-winning first play *The One.*

Participate in our nine-month-long Writers' Labs programme, where we will take you through a three-draft process.

Submit your script to submissions@sohotheatre.com where your play will go directly to our Artistic team.

Invite us to see your show via coverage@sohotheatre.com

We consider every submission for production or any of the further development opportunities.

sohotheatre.com

SUPPORTERS

PRINCIPAL SUPPORTERS
Nicholas Allott OBE
Hani Farsi
Hedley and Fiona
   Goldberg
Michael and Isobel
   Holland
Jack and Linda Keenan
Amelia and Neil
   Mendoza
Lady Susie Sainsbury
Carolyn Ward
Jennifer and Roger
   Wingate

Supporting Partners
Dean Attew
Jo Bennett-Coles
Tamara Box
Matthew Bunting
Stephen Garrett
Beatrice Hollond
Angela Hyde-Courtney
Ian Mill
Phil & Jane Radcliff
Dom & Ali Wallis
Garry Watts

Corporate Supporters
Adnams Southwold
Bargate Murray
Bates Wells &
   Braithwaite
Cameron Mackintosh Ltd
Character Seven
EPIC Private Equity
Financial Express
Fosters
The Groucho Club
John Lewis Oxford Street
Latham & Watkins LLP
Lionsgate UK
The Nadler Hotel
Oberon Books Ltd
Overbury Leisure
Quo Vardis
Richmond Associates
Soho Estates
Soundcraft

Trusts & Foundations
The 29th May 1961
   Charitable Trust
The Andor Charitable
   Trust
Backstage Trust

Bruce Wake Charitable
   Trust
The Boris Karloff
   Charitable Foundation
The Boshier-Hinton
   Foundation
The Buzzacott Stuart
   Defries Memorial Fund
Chapman Charitable
   Trust
The Charles Rifkind
   and Jonathan Levy
   Charitable Settlement
The Charlotte Bonham-
   Carter Charitable Trust
Cockayne – Grants
   for the Arts and The
   London Community
   Foundation
John S Cohen Foundation
The David and Elaine
   Potter Foundation
The D'Oyly Carte
   Charitable Trust
The Eranda Rothschild
   Foundation
The Ernest Cook Trust
Esmée Fairbairn
   Foundation
The Fenton Arts Trust
Fidelio Charitable Trust
Foyle Foundation
Garrick Charitable Trust
The Goldsmiths'
   Company
The Late Mrs Margaret
   Guido's Charitable Trust
Harold Hyam Wingate
   Foundation
Hyde Park Place Estate
   Charity
The Ian Mactaggart Trust
The Idlewild Trust
The John Thaw
   Foundation
John Ellerman
   Foundation
John Lewis Oxford
   Street Community
   Matters Scheme
John Lyon's Charity
JP Getty Jnr Charitable
   Trust
The Kobler Trust
The Leche Trust
The Mackintosh
   Foundation

Mohamed S. Farsi
   Foundation
Noel Coward Foundation
The Peggy Ramsay
   Foundation
The Rose Foundation
The Royal Victoria Hall
   Foundation
Santander Foundation
Schroder Charity Trust
St Giles-in-the-Fields
   and William Shelton
   Educational Charity
The St James's Piccadilly
   Charity
Tallow Chandlers
   Benevolent Fund
The Teale Charitable
   Trust
The Theatres Trust
The Thistle Trust
Unity Theatre Charitable
   Trust
The Wolfson Foundation

Soho Theatre Performance Friends
Rajan Brotia
Alban Gordon
Joe Lam
Andrew Lucas
Walter Ken McCracken
   and Stacie Styles
Mark Whiteley
Gary Wilder

Soho Theatre Playwright Friends
David Aukin
Quentin Bargate
Emily Fletcher
Liam Goddard
Fawn James
John James
Shappi Khorsandi
Jeremy King OBE
David and Linda
   Lakhdhir
Susie Lea
Jonathan Levy
Nick & Annette Mason
Suki Sanhdu OBE
Lesley Symons
Henry Wyndham
Christopher Yu

Soho Theatre Comedy Friends

Kerry Abel
Tiffany Agbeko
Oladipo Agboluaje
Rachel Agustsson
Fran Allen
Matthew Allen
Katherine Andreen
Robert Ash
Adele Ashton
James Atkinson
Valentine Attew
Gabrielle Baigel
Polly Balsom
John Bannister
Zarina Bart
Hannah Barter
Uri Baruchin
Antonio Batista
Ben Battcock
David Baynard
Elaine Becker
Seona Bell
Alex Bertulis-Fernandes
Julia Biro
Sophie Birshan
Kieran Birt
Matthew Boyle
Matthew Bradfield
Christian Braeker
Claire Breen
Christie Brown
Jesse Buckle
Iain Burnett
Oscar Cainer
Lynsey Campbell
Indigo Carnie
Chris Carter
Sabine Chalmers
Deborah Charles
Nicholas Clemmow
Ilya Colak-Antic
Camilla Cole
Vanessa Cook
Grant Court
Eva Culhane
Alli Cunningham
Josephine Curry
Mandy D'Abo
Mark David
Haralambos Dayantis
Sharon Eva Degen
Laura Denholm
Jeff Dormer
Edwina Ellis
Kate Emery
Amanda Farley

Samantha Fennessy
Peter Fenwick
Stephen Ferns
Stephen Fowler
Kevin French
Trevor French
Paul Friedman
John Fry
David Gardner
Cyrus Gilbert-Rolfe
François-Xavier Girard
Cindy Glenn
Kiera Godfrey
Terry Good
Louise Goodman
Robert Grant
Eva Greenspan
Steven Greenwood
Emma Gunnell
Edward Hacking
Gary Haigh
John Hamilton
Colin Hann
Anthony Hawser
Simon Herman
Karen Howlett
John Ireland
Anna Jagric
Nadia Jennings
Clodagh de Jode
Simon Jones
Sue Jones
Toby Jones
Amelia Kenworthy
Matt Kempen
Robert King
Hari Kitching
Julie Knight
Eric Knopp
Andreas Kubat
Michael Kunz
Emily Kyne
Hattie de Laine
Clive Laing
Philip Lawson
Simon Lee
Damien Lefortier
Kerry Jean Lister
Ian Livingston
Nicolaas Luijten
Lucy MacCarthy
Jane Maguire
Marea Maloney
Anthony Marraccino
Amanda Mason
Neil Mawson
Paul McNamee
Jennifer Meech

Laura Meecham
Kosten Metreweli
Mike Miller
Nick Mills
Richard Moore
Nathan Mosher
Maryam Mossavar
Jim Murgatroyd
Mr and Mrs Roger Myddelton
Bianca Nardi
Lena Nguyen
James Nicoll
John O'Keeffe
Samantha O'Sullivan
Sam Owen
Alan Pardoe
Simon Parsonage
Helen Pegrum
Andrew Perkins
Keith Petts
Marijn Poeschmann
Nick Pontt
Dean Reilly
Stephanie Ressort
Charlotte Richardson
Annabel Ridley
Giles Robinette
Antonia Rolph
Dan Rosenberg
Kate Ross
Graeme Rossiter
Tamanna Ruparel
Lauren Rutherford
Rebecca Rycroft
Benjamin Samuel
Ron Sandler
Natalia Siabkin
Beth Silver
Michelle Singer
Amanda Singleton
Christopher Slevin
Hari Sriskantha
Sarah Stanford
Tom Stockton
Jennifer Stott
Barry Street
Christine Styrnau
Catherine Taite
Tracey Tattersall
Daniel Taylor
Sarah Taylor
Victoria Thomas
Andrew Thorne
Anthony Stewart Townson
James Treen
Gabriel Vogt

Elizabeth Vrachimi
Trent Walton
Toby Warren
Thomas Weatherley
Zachary Webb
Sam Webster
Mike Welsh
Peter Westaway
Matt Whitehurst
Luke Wiles
Alexandra Williams
Gareth Williams
Geoff Williams
Kevin Williams
Sion Williams-Eliyesil
Allan Willis
Diana Wilson
Jennifer Wood
Anna Woolgar
Neil Woollard
Laura Wright
Jessie Wyld
Liz Young

We would also like to
thank Yolanda Mercy,
Ifeyinwa Frederick
and those supporters
who wish to remain
anonymous.

The Fleabag Writers'
Bursary is provided
in partnership with
Sceptre.

We are also supported
by Westminster City
Council West End Ward
Budget and the London
Borough of Waltham
Forest.

SHEFF!ELD THEATRES

Sheffield Theatres is home to three theatres: the Crucible, the Sheffield landmark with a world-famous reputation; the Studio, an intimate, versatile space for getting closer to the action; and the gleaming Lyceum, the beautiful proscenium that hosts the best of the UK's touring shows.

Sheffield Theatres won Regional Theatre of the Year at The Stage Awards 2020, for an unprecedented fourth time. With a reputation for outstanding new work, recent hits include new musical STANDING AT THE SKY'S EDGE, with music and lyrics by Mercury Prize nominated Richard Hawley, and a dazzling new adaptation of Yann Martel's multi-million selling LIFE OF PI by Lolita Chakrabarti (opening at London's Wyndham's Theatre in June 2020). This success follows the phenomenal Sheffield musical EVERYBODY'S TALKING ABOUT JAMIE which started life at the Crucible in February 2017, before transferring to the West End later that year.

For 2020, EVERYBODY'S TALKING ABOUT JAMIE starts its UK tour at the Lyceum Theatre, Sheffield Theatres' Artistic Director Robert Hastie adapts and directs Shakespeare's CORIOLANUS in the Crucible, while RUN SISTER RUN starts life in the Studio Theatre.

sheffieldtheatres.co.uk

@crucibletheatre @SheffieldLyceum
Facebook: Sheffield Theatres

Supported using public funding by
ARTS COUNCIL ENGLAND

Sheffield
City Council

SHEFFIELD THEATRES STAFF

Chief Executive Dan Bates
Artistic Director Robert Hastie

SENIOR MANAGEMENT TEAM
Communications & Fundraising Director
Claire Murray
Finance & Resources Director Bookey Oshin
Producer John Tomlinson

ADMINISTRATION TEAM
HR Manager Andrea Ballantyne
HR Officer Lorna Knight
**Assistant to Chief Executive & Artistic
Director** Jackie Pass

BOX OFFICE TEAM
Sales & Customer Care Manager Caroline
Laurent
Deputy Sales Managers
Kate Fisher, Louise Renwick
Sales & Customer Care Supervisor Claire
Fletcher*
Access & Sales Supervisor
Paul Whitley
Sales & Group Supervisor
Ian Caudwell
Sales Assistants Alexandra Brown, Sue
Cooper, Alistair Eades, Sally Field, Charlotte
Keyworth, Faye Hardaker, Pat Holland,
Philip Lee, Rebecca McQuillan, Christine
Monaghan, Heather Reynolds, Soshain
Shehadeh, Christine Smith, Irene Stewart,
Katy Wainwright, Hannah Winnell

COMMUNICATIONS TEAM
Communications Manager Rachel Nutland
Deputy Communications Manager Oliver
Eastwood
Media Officer Ellie Greenfield
Communications Officers Carrie Askew,
Laura Bloor, Hannah Gatward, Anna Lord,
Keir Shields
Communications Trainee Georgina Botham
Programmer Helen Dobson
National Press Support Jo Allan PR

CUSTOMER SERVICES TEAM
General Bars & Catering Manager Andrew
Cooper
House Manager Debbie Smith
Restaurant Manager Mark Headley
Trainee Deputy Restaurant Manager James
Doolan
Head Chef Natalie Bailey
Trainee Sous Chef Daniel Lockwood
Commis Chef Antonio Massuno
Events Manager Lianne Froggatt
Catering & Bars Shift Leaders
Aeddan Lockett, Archie Ward
Café Supervisor Joanne Murrison
Duty Managers Courtney Ball, Sue Cooper,
Andrea Eades, Denise Hobart, Lucy Hockney,
Adrian Tolson, Tracy Waldron

Firepersons Emma Chapman, Susanne
Palzer, Lucy Procter, Heather Reynolds, Jon
Robinson, Joe White
Cellar Person Robin Atkinson **Restaurant
Staff** Curtis Fairest, Katherine Gara, Rachel
Luscombe, William Stroie
Catering Assistants Megan Archer, Carrie
Askew, Olivia Barton, Mia Crook, James
Doolan, Jenny Everson, Fabien O'Farrell, Judi
Flint, Alex Glentworth, Jessica Goh, Joanne
Hall, Nicole Hodder, Jorja Holmes, Sandra
Holmes, Sue Jones, Holly Kempton, Hannah
Lamare, Luke Lincoln, Phoebe Lindley, Joe
Marriot, Liam McGrath, Fionnuala Meely,
Andrea Millen, Sarah Moat, Lois Pearson,
Ioana Radulescu, Cyndi Richardson, Abby
Russell, Louise Sanderson, Liz Sayles, Richard
Sidebottom, Grace Parker-Slater, Grace
Smith, Claire Sweeney, Jonathon Syer, Caryl
Thomas
Front of House Assistants Anne Archer,
Hester Astell, Steve Athey, Courtney Ball,
Belinda Beasley, Marianne Bolton, George
Bowley, Lauren Browes, Mari Bullock, Ann
Butler, Lorna Byrne, Julie Cartwright, Jane
Challenger, Emma Chapman, Lilli Connelly,
Vicky Cooper, Gillian Crossland, John
Daggett, Marie Darling, Sandra Eddison,
Connie Fiddament, Maureen Foster, Jake
Goode, Samantha Green, Nick Henry,
Rebecca Hill, Denise Hobart, Lucy Hockney,
Tilly Ireson, Scott Johnson, Beth Kinross,
Alex Lamb, Martha Lamb, Diane Lilleyman,
Margaret Lindley, Harry Foster-Major,
Aimee Marshall, Christine Monaghan, Sylvia
Mortimer, Susie Newman, Kourtney Owen,
Liz Owen, Susanne Palzer, Holly Parker,
Jodie Passey, Ann Phenix, Lucy Procter,
Richard Rawson, Heather Reynolds, Jonathan
Robinson, Irene Stewart, Dionne Sulph,
Daniel Thorpe, Adrian Tolson, Bev Turner,
Tracy Waldron, Christine Wallace, Joe White,
Stuart Williamson

FACILITIES TEAM
Buildings Manager John Bates
Buildings Officer Rob Chapman
Maintenance Supervisor Julian Simpson
Maintenance Technician Richard Powell-
Pepper
House Assistants Adam Battey, David Hayes,
Amy Jenner, James McCready, Jacob Ross,
Kate Wilkinson, Richard Winks
Receptionist/Telephonist Angela Ridgeway
Head Cleaners Jenny Hardy,
Tracey Kemp
Cleaners Susan Baxter, Louisa Cottingham,
Yvonne Dwyer, Gail Fox, Jill Francis, Lynn
Highton, Pamela Jackson, Diane Sayles,
Diane Turton, Karen Walker, Andrew Wild

THANKS

Franc Ashman, Karl Queensborough, Esther Hall, Jason Barnett,
Monica Dolan, Ria Zmitrowicz, Edward Bluemel, Janisè Sadik, Kate
Wasserberg, Deirdre O'Halloran, Matt Xia, Katie Posner, David Luff,
Mark Godfrey, Jules Haworth, Holly De Angelis, Lakesha Arie-Angelo,
Gill Greer, Ruby Clarke, Rob Hastie, Alan Carroll, Gabriel Bisset-Smith,
Ric Renton, Ross Willis, Abbi Greenland and Patch.

RUN SISTER RUN

Chloë Moss

Acknowledgements

Special thanks and love to: Mel Kenyon, Charlotte Bennett,
Katie Posner and all at Paines Plough, Sarah Dickenson,
Ken Moss, Patricia Moss, Nick Moss, Tim Price, Franklin Moss
Price, Martha Moss Price, Colette Kane, Phoebe-Chi Kane-
Moss, Oliver Kane-Rice, Joshua Kane-Rice. Many thanks also
to Sarah Frankcom, Suzanne Bell, Pam James, all at Soho
Theatre and Sheffield Crucible.

C.M.

For you, Dad.

I love you, I love you, I love you, I love you…

4

Characters

CONNIE, *various ages*
URSULA, *various ages*
ADRIAN, *various ages*
JACK, *various ages*

Note on the Text

A forward slash in the text (/) indicates a character changing tack.

A dash in the text (–) indicates another character interrupting, or overlapping speech.

This text went to press before the end of rehearsals and so may differ slightly from the play as performed.

ONE

2020. The park. A sunny afternoon. CONNIE *(early fifties) sits on a park bench holding an ice cream in each hand.*

She waits.

TWO

2019. A large living room. Vases of flowers dotted around. CONNIE *enters. She is loaded down with more bunches of flowers. She kneels down and starts to arrange the new flowers into the vases, searching for space between stems and cramming them in.*

The noise of the front door opening and slamming shut.

CONNIE. Jack?

    Silence.

    Jack?

    JACK *(nineteen) appears.*

JACK. Yeah?

CONNIE. What are you doing here?

JACK. I live here.

CONNIE. I thought you were out tonight.

JACK. Well, I'm back. Is that okay?

CONNIE. Of course. *(Beat.)* Come into the room. I'm not radioactive.

    JACK *huffs and steps forward.*

Have you been crying?

JACK. No I haven't been *crying*.

CONNIE. Your eyes look red.

JACK (*about the flowers*). Fucking hay fever probably. What happened to the old people's home?

CONNIE. They won't accept them any more. Health and safety. One of the residents smashed a vase against the wall. (*Beat.*) Can't let them go to waste.

JACK. Why don't you just give them to people in the street?

CONNIE. Claudia wouldn't be very happy, would she? Old people's home's different. Community thing. Who'd bother coming into the shop if they knew come half-five I'd start handing out free bunches of flowers. Put her out of business.

JACK *sits*.

JACK (*beat. Off* CONNIE). What?

CONNIE. Sure you're okay?

JACK. Give it a rest, Mum.

CONNIE. Why aren't you staying out?

JACK. Talk about making someone feel fucking unwelcome in their own home.

CONNIE. That's a ridiculous thing to say. You told me you were staying at Kate's and now you're not. How can you inflate that to me wishing you didn't live here any more? It's very dramatic.

ADRIAN (*late fifties*) *enters*.

ADRIAN. *I* wish you didn't live here any more.

JACK. Trust me. I don't *want* to live here. I'm trying. Got a job, haven't I?

ADRIAN. Work experience.

JACK. An *internship*. Do you know how many people applied for it?

CONNIE. And we're really proud of you.

ADRIAN. You didn't apply. I arranged it for you.

JACK. And I'm fucking *doing* it. What d'you want... blood? (*Beat.*) It's demoralising. Being trapped here.

CONNIE. Nobody's trapping you, love.

ADRIAN. Door's right behind you.

CONNIE. Adrian –

JACK. D'you want me to get on my hands and knees and bow down in gratitude to you both?

CONNIE. Oh come on –

ADRIAN. Thought we were shot of you tonight anyway –

CONNIE. Adrian –

JACK. It's over. She dumped me.

ADRIAN. Kate?

JACK. Yes. Kate. My girlfriend. *Ex*-girlfriend.

CONNIE. Oh love, I'm sorry.

JACK. Don't be, she's a fucking *bitch*.

ADRIAN. I didn't have the best feeling about her, I've got to say.

CONNIE. I thought she seemed great.

ADRIAN. I think I'm better at reading people the older I get.

CONNIE. You only met her once.

ADRIAN. Exactly. (*Beat.*) Another boy is it?

JACK. No.

ADRIAN. What then?

    Beat.

JACK. She doesn't think we're 'right' together.

ADRIAN. Fuck's sake.

JACK. I know.

    Beat.

CONNIE. Maybe, you weren't... 'right' together.

ADRIAN. Connie, don't go getting involved for Christ's sake.

CONNIE. I'm not getting involved, I'm just pointing out –

JACK. Yeah well, no offence, Mum, but you've only met her like twice –

CONNIE. Four times.

JACK. Okay four fucking times. But you don't know anything about it. About *us*.

CONNIE. I know that… as a rule, if somebody ends a relationship with someone because they don't think they're 'right' together then it's a fairly safe bet they're not 'right' together.

Silence. JACK *stands, furious. He punches the wall.*

ADRIAN. Well done, Connie.

JACK. I need to get out.

ADRIAN. Why don't you then? Go and see your friends. Drown your sorrows.

CONNIE. Adrian –

ADRIAN. What?

JACK. I haven't got any money.

ADRIAN. You only had your allowance four days ago.

JACK. It was a statement of fact. I'm not asking for anything.

Beat. ADRIAN *pulls a wallet from his pocket and counts out a couple of notes. He hands them to* JACK *who looks down at them. Beat.* ADRIAN *takes another note out and hands that over.*

ADRIAN. That's your lot.

JACK *tucks the notes into his pocket.*

CONNIE. Be careful. (*Beat.*) You know what I mean.

JACK *smirks.*

It's not funny, Jack. I'm not stupid, I know what goes on.

JACK. What goes on then?

CONNIE. Cocaine, Ecstasy…

JACK. Blast and Ket for me actually.

ADRIAN. Don't rise to it, Connie.

CONNIE. Jack, I know you must be –

JACK. Oh, don't do the 'I know you're in pain' speech. *Please*. Makes me wanna vomit. (*Beat*.) I'm not in pain.

CONNIE. I know you liked her. There's nothing wrong with feeling up–

JACK. She's pregnant.

Beat.

ADRIAN. Oh *fucking* hell. Here we go.

CONNIE. Are you sure?

JACK. She did a test. I saw it. Two lines.

Beat.

ADRIAN. Is it yours?

JACK. Yes.

ADRIAN. How d'you know?

JACK. Because she's not like that.

CONNIE. Like *what*?

ADRIAN. Jesus fucking wept.

Silence. JACK *slumps down into an armchair*.

CONNIE. Do her parents know?

JACK. No.

ADRIAN. Is she going private? I'll pay for it. Tell her I'll pay.

JACK. She won't go private.

ADRIAN. No of course she won't. Bloody… capitalist hippies. Four-by-four in the drive and a Filipino living in the cellar but don't take any pressure off the NHS for God's sake. Show you're a man of the people. (*Beat*.) Music, isn't it?

CONNIE. What are you talking about, Adrian?

ADRIAN. Her father. Something to do with music.

CONNIE. What's her father got to do with it?

ADRIAN. Marches to save the planet then jets off to LA.
  Drinks fucking kombucha.

JACK. She doesn't *want* to go private.

ADRIAN. Fantastic principles. Drag it out for as long as
  possible. All the while there's a *baby* developing –

CONNIE. It's not a baby.

ADRIAN. What the fuck is it then?

CONNIE. A *fetus*. (*Beat*.) It's her decision whether to go
  privately or not. It's nothing to do with us –

ADRIAN. We're the gran–

CONNIE. We're *not* grandparents. Stay out of it. It's her body –

JACK. She wants to keep it.

CONNIE. What?

JACK. She's keeping it.

  Silence.

  D'you really think I'd have told you if she was having an
  abortion? (*Pause*.) She said she'll do it on her own if I don't
  want to be involved.

  Beat.

CONNIE. And do you?

JACK. Do I what?

CONNIE. Want to be *involved*.

ADRIAN. He's *nineteen* for Christ's sake.

CONNIE. Jack?

JACK. No. I do not want to be a fucking father.

  Silence.

CONNIE. Adrian?

  ADRIAN *raises his hands and walks out of the room.*
  CONNIE *and* JACK *sit in silence.*

  Is she religious?

JACK *scoffs*.

JACK. No. She *was* going to get an abortion but then she saw this account on Instagram where the mother and baby wear exactly the same thing all the time, it's called '*twinning*' apparently and she changed her mind. Basically she wants a fucking doll.

Beat.

CONNIE. She's very young. She needs support.

JACK. Why should I *support* someone who's just *dumped* me?

CONNIE. She needs you to be –

JACK. She doesn't *need* me to be anything, that's the whole point… she just fucking finished with me. When's that gonna land?

CONNIE. She's frightened.

JACK. What about *me*?

CONNIE. The world doesn't revolve around you, Jack. That might come as a shock –

JACK. Oh fuck off.

CONNIE slaps JACK.

CONNIE. I'm sorry. I'm so sorry.

CONNIE goes to him and puts her arms around him.

JACK. Get off me.

CONNIE. No. Let me give you a hug.

JACK. I don't want a hug.

CONNIE. Please. I'm sorry. I'm so…

JACK lets CONNIE hug him.

It'll be alright. Whatever happens. It'll be alright. I promise you.

Silence.

JACK. She spouted this… *bullshit*… about wanting 'a proper connection' to someone. She's been reading this fucking self-help book. (*Beat*.) Like her and I don't have a connection? What the fuck's that about?

Pause. JACK *puts his head in his hands and starts to cry.*

CONNIE. It will. It'll be okay.

JACK *sinks into her.* CONNIE *wraps her arms around him. Silence.*

When you were tiny, I'd sit and hold you like this for entire days. Shut the curtains, get on the sofa... whole days. Literally did nothing else apart from feed us both, go to the loo and just... breathe you in.

Beat.

JACK. Was that because you had postnatal depression?

Beat.

CONNIE. I didn't have postnatal depression. (*Beat*.) Where did you get that from?

Beat. The door opens and ADRIAN *walks in. As soon as he does* JACK *springs away from* CONNIE.

ADRIAN. We'll sort this out. Don't worry.

ADRIAN *pours a drink.*

If she thinks she can emotionally blackmail you –

CONNIE. She's not trying to –

ADRIAN. Connie, let me fucking speak.

Silence.

She's supposed to be going away to university in September, isn't she? (*Off* JACK *nodding*.) Well, that's out of the window with a kid, isn't it?

CONNIE. Not necessarily.

ADRIAN. Live in halls with her, will it? Go to lectures in a papoose? (*Beat*.) Where's she going?

JACK. Edinburgh.

ADRIAN. Edinburgh. Perfect. That'll work out brilliantly.

JACK. She might change her mind. She always changes her mind.

ADRIAN. Of course she'll change her fucking mind. She's playing you.

CONNIE. Why would she be playing him?

ADRIAN. Give it a few days. Some space. No contact. (*Beat.*) Let's all just... exhale.

Beat. JACK *nods.* ADRIAN *takes another swig of his drink then reaches for his wallet again. He pulls out two more notes and hands them to* JACK.

Put it in a box for now. We'll deal with it.

JACK *nods. He stands.*

JACK. I'll call Arthur.

ADRIAN. Pace yourself.

JACK *nods.*

See you tomorrow.

CONNIE *stands and hugs* JACK, *he pulls away.*

JACK. See you tomorrow.

JACK *leaves the room. Silence.*

ADRIAN *drains his glass and pours another.*

ADRIAN. D'you want a drink?

CONNIE *shakes her head. Silence*

She'll change her mind. (*Beat.*) It'll be alright. *He'll* be alright. He's a tough boy. Got that mindset. (*Beat.*) Nobody's died. We'll sort it.

CONNIE *watches as* ADRIAN *tops up his glass.*

Have a drink.

CONNIE. I don't want a drink.

ADRIAN. Calm your nerves.

CONNIE. My nerves are calm.

ADRIAN *starts to pour* CONNIE *a drink.*

I don't want a fucking drink, Adrian.

He stops and puts the glass down. Beat.

ADRIAN. What's the mother like?

CONNIE....

ADRIAN. The *girl's* mother –

CONNIE. *Kate.*

ADRIAN. You met her didn't you?

CONNIE (*nodding*). She seemed nice.

ADRIAN. Why don't you call her?

CONNIE. Why would I call her?

ADRIAN. The longer she leaves it.

CONNIE. I'm *not* calling her mother.

ADRIAN. She needs someone to talk some common sense
into her.

CONNIE. *Common sense.*

ADRIAN. Yes. Common fucking sense. Do me a favour,
Connie... can you drop the sisterhood routine for two seconds
please and think about the impact this could have on Jack?

Silence. CONNIE *stares at* ADRIAN. *He takes another swig
of his drink.*

She won't go through with it anyway. Of course she won't.

Silence. ADRIAN *drinks.*

Oh don't do this.

CONNIE. Do what? What am I doing?

ADRIAN. The morose silence.

CONNIE. I'm just thinking, Adrian. Is that allowed?

ADRIAN. *What* are you thinking?

CONNIE. I'm *thinking* about Ursula. Actually.

ADRIAN. The morose silence followed by the non sequitur.
Classic. God give me fucking strength.

Pause.

CONNIE. I've dreamt about her every night this week. (*Beat*.) Haven't dreamt about her in years and then… four nights in a row. I knew something was wrong

ADRIAN. So what? You dreamt about your sister. I have recurring dreams about Ian Botham but I don't think he's travelled through some astral plane to offer me guidance on my outswing. What exactly are you saying, my love? Do you want me to buy you a dream catcher?

CONNIE. Don't say 'my love' when you're being like that.

ADRIAN. Being like what?

CONNIE. A cunt.

Pause.

ADRIAN. D'you know your problem, Connie?

CONNIE. Yes I do. I know exactly what my problem is.

ADRIAN. You can't handle a crisis. You go to pieces. And it's not even your fault actually. It's an… accumulation –

CONNIE. Yes. Exactly that –

ADRIAN. All that *baggage*. You're completely stymied. You can't… separate things out… *compartmentalise*.

CONNIE. No, I can't, Adrian.

ADRIAN. Can't *rationalise*. (*Beat*.) It's not even your fault.

CONNIE. No you're right, it's not.

ADRIAN. But you have to / you do have to be strong. For Jack.

Pause.

CONNIE. Put it in a box.

Beat.

ADRIAN. Yes. Put it in a fucking box.

ADRIAN walks out. CONNIE picks up ADRIAN's glass and spits in it, a second later he walks back in the room for his drink. CONNIE hands him the glass, he takes a swig and walks back out.

CONNIE *stays*.

THREE

2010. The bedroom. CONNIE *applies make-up over a black eye, sponging on a thick layer of foundation. She has a wine bottle and a glass next to her on the dressing table.*

ADRIAN *enters in boxer shorts and a shirt, drinking from a whisky glass. He drains the glass and puts it down to pull on a pair of trousers.*

CONNIE. Is he asleep?

ADRIAN. Just about.

CONNIE. Did you read him a story?

Beat.

ADRIAN. Yes.

CONNIE *stops.*

CONNIE. You didn't, did you?

ADRIAN....

CONNIE. If he doesn't get a story he won't settle properly.

ADRIAN. He's settled.

CONNIE. He'll be up. He needs a story. And his night light. Did you put his night light on?

ADRIAN. What night light?

CONNIE. It's plugged straight into the socket on the wall. It's a little pig's head.

ADRIAN. He's got to get used to the dark.

CONNIE. Why?

ADRIAN. *Why?*

CONNIE. Most children his age are scared of the dark.

ADRIAN. Oh stop it. He's not a baby, Connie.

CONNIE. He's *my* baby.

ADRIAN. You shouldn't call him a baby. It's infantilising. Makes him *act* like a baby. All these fucking imaginary friends. We should take him to see someone.

CONNIE. He's nine.

ADRIAN. Exactly. When I was nine –

CONNIE. When you were nine you wore hobnailed boots and hair trousers. And your father made you plough the fields of your country pile.

Beat. CONNIE *fills her glass.*

He's sensitive.

CONNIE *picks up a strip of pills from the dressing table, she pops one out and swallows it with the wine.*

ADRIAN. Shouldn't you think about coming off them? (*Beat.*) Can't be good. All these years.

CONNIE. Probably not. (*Beat.*) Fasten this for me.

Pause. CONNIE *hands* ADRIAN *a silver locket for him to put around her neck. He fiddles with the clasp.*

ADRIAN. This is like something out of a cracker. Spent a fortune on pearls, I've never seen you wearing them.

CONNIE. Pearls are bad luck.

ADRIAN. My bad luck. Money down the drain.

CONNIE. It's sentimental.

ADRIAN *reads a name on the locket.*

ADRIAN. Who is Doreen anyway?

CONNIE *tucks the necklace under her collar.*

CONNIE. My auntie. I tell you that every time you ask.

ADRIAN. You never talk about her.

CONNIE. You want to hear about my Auntie Doreen? (*Beat.*) What's the wife called again?

ADRIAN. Claudia.

CONNIE. Claudia. Claudia. Claudia.

ADRIAN. She's a florist. Hobby job really. Just opened a shop, ask her about that. (*Beat.*) They asked us around to theirs on Saturday as well. I said yes.

CONNIE. Bit much, isn't it? Twice in a week.

ADRIAN. It's an annual thing they do. For some charity.

CONNIE. What charity?

ADRIAN. I don't know. Starving llamas. There's a posh raffle. Last year somebody won afternoon tea with Ralph Fiennes.

CONNIE. Sounds fantastic. (*Beat.*) But I can't go.

Beat.

ADRIAN. Why not?

Beat.

CONNIE. I've got a job.

ADRIAN. A *job*?

CONNIE. Yes.

ADRIAN. Since when?

CONNIE. Since last week.

Silence. CONNIE takes a glug of wine.

Have you got a problem with that?

ADRIAN. I haven't got a *problem* with it. It's just a bit sudden, that's all.

CONNIE. A bit sudden?

ADRIAN. Out of the blue. (*Beat.*) I suppose it's a shock.

CONNIE. I've got a job, Adrian. I haven't grown a cock.

Beat.

ADRIAN. So what is it then? This secret job?

CONNIE. It's not a secret.

ADRIAN. Presumably you went for an interview?

CONNIE. Yes I went for an interview.

ADRIAN. And before the interview you saw it advertised?

Beat.

CONNIE. No. Somebody told me about it.

ADRIAN. Okay. (*Beat*.) Somebody told you about it.

CONNIE. Can you get to the point?

ADRIAN. The point is that one might usually mention going for an interview.

CONNIE. One didn't want to mention it. One felt nervous. One thought one wouldn't get it.

ADRIAN. But you did.

CONNIE. Yes I did.

ADRIAN. Course you did.

CONNIE. Don't patronise me.

ADRIAN. How is that patronising? How is having faith in my wife patronising?

CONNIE. Because you don't know what it is.

ADRIAN. What is it?

Beat.

CONNIE. I'm an usher at the cinema.

Beat.

ADRIAN. What do you mean?

CONNIE. I mean I'm an usher at the cinema. Taking tickets, showing people to the seats and – the best bit – selling ice cream in one of those trays with a strap that goes around your neck.

ADRIAN. Okay. Hilarious. What job have you got really?

CONNIE. I'm an usher at the cinema.

ADRIAN. Connie.

CONNIE. I'm not lying, why would I lie?

ADRIAN. Because you *enjoy* winding me up.

CONNIE. No I don't.

ADRIAN. You do. This is typical. Ten minutes, they're due in ten minutes.

CONNIE. What's my new job got to do with the fact that we've got guests arriving?

ADRIAN. My *boss*.

CONNIE. Yes?

ADRIAN. We're pulling out all the stops –

CONNIE. A leg of lamb and some tiramisu –

ADRIAN. There's a lot riding on tonight. A possible *promotion*… it's stressful enough as it is and then you suddenly announce you've got a job in the cinema as a fucking usher.

CONNIE. I'm not working tonight if that's what you're worried about?

ADRIAN. Don't… Connie.

CONNIE. I'm… genuinely / I'm confused.

ADRIAN. You're not confused. Do yourself a favour and fucking… zip it. Do not mention it tonight. We'll talk tomorrow. (*About the wine.*) And you can knock that on the head.

> ADRIAN *picks the bottle up,* CONNIE *snatches it back.*

Actually, we can talk about it now. You're not doing it. There we go. Done.

CONNIE. I am doing it.

ADRIAN. No you're not.

CONNIE. I've already done it.

> *Beat.* ADRIAN *stops. He turns to face* CONNIE. *She takes a swig from the bottle.*

Wednesday evening. I had a trial shift. It went really well. They were delighted with me. Apparently I sold more ice-cream tubs in that one shift than they usually do for an entire Saturday night. It's just about engaging with people. I spoke to this one woman, she was eighty-four, goes to watch a film every week on her own. I didn't charge her, you'd think she won the lottery. (*Beat*.) I had a really lovely time. (*Off* ADRIAN.) What?

Beat.

ADRIAN. You're a PR manager.

CONNIE. No, I'm not. I haven't done that for over nine years. (*Beat*.) I'm an *usher* in the cinema.

ADRIAN. I appreciate your confidence is probably shot to pieces. After all this time. Out of the game.

CONNIE. My confidence is fine. I left the game because I didn't like the game. I'm not 'out' of it. 'Out' implies I've been excluded. I'm not excluded. I left entirely of my own volition.

Silence.

ADRIAN. Did anyone see you?

CONNIE. Where?

ADRIAN. Wednesday night. In the *cinema*.

CONNIE. Lots of people saw me.

ADRIAN. Anyone we know. Don't be a smart arse.

CONNIE. I spotted one of the mothers from school but she didn't see me. The uniform's the same colour as the walls so you're sort of camouflaged.

Beat.

ADRIAN. Claudia needs help apparently. You could do a couple of mornings with her.

CONNIE. I don't want to work in a florist, Adrian.

ADRIAN. You love flowers.

CONNIE. You love whisky. Go and work in a fucking off-licence.

ADRIAN. I can't say sorry any more than I have already. If this is some sort of punishment –

CONNIE. Getting a job in a cinema is punishing you? Trust me, I can think of much better ways –

ADRIAN grabs CONNIE by the hair.

ADRIAN. You will not fucking embarrass me tonight. You will not fucking embarrass me. You're not working in a cinema selling ice creams. I said I was sorry. You accepted my apology. Don't play games with me, you silly fucking cow. Grow up and move on.

ADRIAN lets go. CONNIE staggers forward. JACK stands there. CONNIE plasters on a smile.

CONNIE. Hello, Munchkin.

ADRIAN walks out. JACK stares at CONNIE.

You okay, sweetheart?

The front door slams. Silence.

Jack?

JACK. I couldn't sleep because Dad didn't put the night light on and I was thirsty so I got up and went downstairs.

CONNIE. Come on, back into bed.

JACK. Then I saw someone in the garden so I went outside. It's my new friend.

CONNIE. What friend? (*Beat.*) Is it Mr Tum Tum?

JACK shakes his head.

JACK. It's a girl.

CONNIE. Mrs Eyes-Are-Brown?

JACK shakes his head.

JACK. She's waiting in the living room. Can I bring her up?

CONNIE. Yes please. I'd love to meet her, darling.

JACK leaves. CONNIE sinks onto the bed, rubbing her head. She wipes her eyes in the mirror. After a minute or so, JACK reappears with URSULA (forty), holding her hand.

JACK. This is my Auntie Ursula.

CONNIE stops, completely shocked. Instinctively she steps towards URSULA as if she might throw her arms around her in relief. She stops herself.

Pause.

URSULA. He was out in the garden. I was at the gate. I wasn't even going to come in.

Pause. CONNIE gathers herself, almost like she's emerging from a trance. She notices for the first time that JACK has tight hold of URSULA's hand.

CONNIE. Sweetheart, do you want to go and climb back in bed? I'll be through in a minute, go on.

JACK stays. URSULA stares at him.

Now. Go on, Jack.

JACK leaves. Silence.

URSULA. He's absolutely beautiful.

CONNIE. What / what are you doing here?

URSULA. I wasn't going to come in –

CONNIE. You were at the gate.

URSULA. I wasn't... I was passing –

CONNIE. Passing?

URSULA. I stopped for a second and there he was –

CONNIE. You can't be here, Ursula. Not now. You have to go. I do want to / I want to see you but I can't –

URSULA. I know. I wasn't intending / I didn't intend to –

CONNIE. There's people coming.

Beat. URSULA nods. She stays put. Both still staring at one another.

Is something wrong? (*Beat.*) Are you ill?

URSULA. I don't think so. (*Beat.*) No. No. I'm not. I'm okay. In fact I'm well. Really well... actually. Things are –

CONNIE. Good. That's –

URSULA. Wasn't even sure you still lived here. I didn't even / he just put his hand out. Next minute he's dragging me up the path. Funny, isn't he? Confident. You should watch him with strangers.

Beat.

CONNIE. I do watch him with strangers.

URSULA. No, yeah I wasn't suggesting that you didn't. Just, y'know… Kids are so trusting. It's a beautiful thing. Shame we have to knock that out of them but you can't take any chances, can you?

CONNIE. No. You can't.

CONNIE takes a swig of wine from her glass. URSULA watches.

This is…

URSULA. It was very… spur of the moment.

CONNIE. We've got people coming. For dinner.

URSULA. Listen to you. (*Beat.*) 'People coming for dinner' and I'm stood here with an… Asda bag.

Silence. CONNIE and URSULA stand looking at one another.

JACK enters carrying a toy rabbit.

CONNIE. Jack.

URSULA. Oh… hello. Who's this then?

JACK. Mr Smith.

JACK holds the rabbit out and URSULA takes it.

URSULA. Hello, Mr Smith, it's lovely to meet you.

JACK. I'm a bit old for him now but I had him since I was born so he's *sentimental*.

URSULA holds the rabbit to her ear.

URSULA. Mr Smith! That's bloody disgustin'! I'll wash your mouth out with soap and water if you say anything like that again. (*To* JACK.) Is he always like this or what?

JACK laughs. URSULA meets CONNIE's gaze.

I've got to go now, Mr Smith. You potty-mouthed beggar. But I'll come back and see you soon. (*Beat.*) Yes… I promise I will.

URSULA *hands the rabbit to* JACK.

CONNIE. Sweetheart, go and get in bed now please.

Beat. JACK *stays where he is, staring up at* URSULA.

Now, Jack.

URSULA. Go on. Be a good boy for your mum, yeah?

URSULA *ruffles* JACK*'s hair and he reluctantly leaves.*

Silence.

What happened to your eye?

CONNIE. I fell over.

URSULA. It looks nasty.

CONNIE. Looks worse than it is. Clumsy aren't I?

URSULA. Are you?

CONNIE. You do look well you look really well. (*Beat.*)
Ursula, I'll call you I will but you do have to go –

URSULA. Connie. Are you okay?

CONNIE. Yes. I'm fine. We've got people coming –

URSULA. Can I see you though?

CONNIE. Yes. Yeah. We'll meet up –

The doorbell goes.

Oh fuck. Fuck fuck fuck. (*Beat.*) Stay here, I'll be back in
a minute.

URSULA *watches as* CONNIE *gulps down the rest of her
wine then looks in the mirror, wipes her eyes and hurriedly
applies lipstick before running out.*

Beat.

URSULA *looks around the room. She moves tentatively over
to the dressing table, picks up the nearly empty bottle of wine
then looks through* CONNIE*'s stuff. She doesn't hear* JACK
enter behind her. He stands watching for a couple of seconds.

JACK. Are you really my auntie?

URSULA *turns quickly.*

URSULA. Give me a fright then.

JACK. Why?

URSULA. 'Cause I never heard you come in. Did you magic
yourself through that door? Have you got special powers?

JACK *nods.* URSULA *goes and sits down on the bed.*

Have you? I thought so. Soon as I saw you, I thought he's
magic that one. What else can you do?

Beat.

JACK. Go invisible.

URSULA (*looking around*). Who said that?

JACK *laughs.*

JACK. Are you though?

URSULA. Am I what?

JACK. My auntie.

URSULA. Yes. Yes I am. (*Beat.*) Me and your mummy are
sisters.

JACK. I haven't got any sisters or brothers.

Beat.

URSULA. Y'know why that is, don't you?

JACK *shakes his head.*

'Cause when you were born, your mum took one look at you
and she went 'Well, I can't top that... he's got superpowers.
It's not fair if I have another one, they're gonna feel
rubbish... next to him.'

JACK. No she didn't.

URSULA. She did. Ask her.

Beat.

JACK. How come we never see you?

Pause.

URSULA. Because... that's just the way it is sometimes. (*Beat*.) With families.

Pause. JACK *considers this. He's satisfied.*

Silence.

JACK. Do you want to see my room?

Beat.

URSULA. No / I mean I would... of course I would but we'd best wait here hey? (*Beat*.) For your mum.

He sits on the bed right next to URSULA. *She stares ahead, suddenly self-conscious.*

JACK. Do you know the dinosaur with the longest name?

URSULA. I don't.

JACK. It's Micropachycephalosaurus.

URSULA. Wow.

JACK. It means 'small-headed lizard'. I know loads of facts about dinosaurs.

URSULA. Do you?

JACK. I've got fifty-four in my room. On the shelves. They're not *life-size* or anything.

URSULA. Oh right.

JACK. Obviously.

Beat.

URSULA. You're a lucky boy you, aren't you?

JACK *shrugs*.

Fifty-four dinosaurs. Lovely big house. (*Beat*.) Bet you love it, don't you? Living here. Must be brilliant? Is it brilliant?

JACK. I've never lived anywhere else so I don't really know. (*Beat*.) My dad says I'm too old. For dinosaurs. Not living here. (*Beat*.) And Mr Smith. I got golf clubs for my birthday. I wanted a dog but my mum said no. We're going to play together on the weekend.

URSULA. D'you like golf?

JACK. I don't know yet. (*Beat.*) D'you know what a birdie is?

URSULA. Little creature with a beak and feathers.

JACK. It's a golfing term.

URSULA. Right.

JACK. My dad gave me a book. I'm trying to learn some stuff before Sunday.

URSULA. You're a clever boy I bet.

JACK. I'm average.

URSULA. No you're not. I can tell you're not.

JACK. I am really. In my class I am.

URSULA. I don't think you are.

JACK. You don't know me.

Silence.

Auntie Ursula?

URSULA. Yes?

JACK. What's a wanker?

Long pause.

URSULA. Where'd you get that from?

JACK. Mummy.

URSULA. What did she / how did it... come up?

JACK. She was arguing with Dad. I was in the wardrobe.

URSULA. Why were you in the wardrobe?

JACK (*shrugs*). I just go in there sometimes. If there's shouting. Is it rude?

Beat.

URSULA. No. No it's not rude.

JACK. Then why won't you tell me?

URSULA. I will tell you.

Beat.

JACK. Go on then.

Beat.

URSULA. It's a gardening… thing. Does he like gardening, your dad?

JACK. No. We've got a man who does it.

URSULA. I dunno. Maybe she was being sarcastic. Because he doesn't do any gardening.

JACK. It sounded sarcastic.

URSULA. There you go. How's school?

JACK. What sort of gardening thing?

Beat.

URSULA. It's like a thing… to dig up soil.

JACK. A trowel?

URSULA. Yes. But bigger.

JACK. A spade.

URSULA. In between a trowel and a spade. It's that.

JACK *is satisfied.*

I have to go now when your mum comes back up.

JACK. Why?

URSULA. Because you've got people, haven't you? Round for *dinner.*

JACK. Will you come back?

Beat.

URSULA. Would you like me to come back?

JACK *nods.*

Would you?

JACK. Yeah.

Silence. URSULA *stares at* JACK *for a few moments. As if stopping herself from reaching for him, she stands and starts to head to the door.*

URSULA. Maybe your mum's waiting for me to go down.
I should go and see –

JACK. I don't like school.

URSULA. Don't you?

JACK. I hate it.

URSULA *turns back towards* JACK.

URSULA. Right. How come?

JACK. There's these boys.

URSULA. What boys?

JACK. Some boys. In school.

URSULA. What about them? What do they do?

JACK. Call me stuff. Names.

URSULA. Do they do anything else? Do they hit you?

Silence.

Have you told anyone?

JACK *shakes his head.*

Why not?

JACK *shrugs.*

You've got to tell someone. Your mum or dad. A teacher.

JACK. Snitches get stitches.

URSULA. If some little shit / if someone's bullying you –

JACK. You grit your teeth and get on with it.

URSULA. No you don't. Who told you that?

Silence. URSULA *sits back down on the bed next to* JACK.

JACK. I do this thing, when I want to cry sometimes. I pinch
my leg at the top. Really hard until it bruises. You'd think
that would *make* you cry wouldn't you? But it doesn't, it

stops it. (*Beat*.) I pinch and it hurts… it does hurt but it takes my mind away.

URSULA. You don't wanna take your mind away. You've got a brilliant little mind you have. I can tell. You wanna keep it safe.

JACK (*shrugs*). Makes me feel better. For a bit.

URSULA. That's no good, that's no good at all. You don't wanna do that.

Silence.

D'you know what I do? When I feel like that.

JACK. Do you feel like that too?

URSULA. Sometimes. Course I do. Everyone feels like that sometimes.

JACK. Do they?

URSULA. Yes.

JACK. Even the Queen?

URSULA. 'Specially the Queen. Got a helluva lot on her plate, hasn't she? All them corgis… all that waving. (*Beat*.) You know what I do when I feel like that? (*Beat*.) I go like this. I get my arms and I wrap them round myself like I'm giving myself a great big hug and I close my eyes and I say 'I love you I love you I love you I love you' just quietly. And you feel a bit silly at first especially when you're my age but then it starts feeling alright and it's better than doing that… hurting yourself.

Silence.

You think I'm crackers, don't you? D'you know what? I am a bit crackers. But that's alright as well. Everyone's a little bit crackers. Why don't you give it a go? I'll do it first. You can laugh at me if you like, I don't mind.

Beat. JACK *stares up at* URSULA. *She wraps her arms around herself closes her eyes and starts to chant under her breath.*

I love you I love you I love you I love you I love you.

URSULA *opens her eyes.*

Are you laughing at me?

JACK *shakes his head.* URSULA *continues. After a moment* JACK *follows and wraps his arms around himself, closing his eyes shut.*

Keep them shut.

As he does so URSULA *opens hers and watches* JACK. *They both chant 'I love you' together, quietly.*

CONNIE *appears in the doorway, wine glass in hand. She stands watching for a few moments.*

CONNIE. Jack. Get into bed please.

JACK *looks up startled. Self-conscious.*

Now.

URSULA *nods at* JACK, *she goes in for a hug but* CONNIE *pulls him away.*

JACK. Bye, Auntie Ursula.

Beat.

URSULA. Bye bye, sweetheart.

JACK *stays.* CONNIE *ushers him out of the room then shuts the door.*

CONNIE. What the fuck was that about?

Beat.

URSULA. He's getting bullied. In school.

CONNIE. Did he tell you that?

URSULA. Yes.

CONNIE. We've been in. It's been sorted out.

URSULA. He didn't seem to think it'd been sorted out.

CONNIE. It has. It's stopped now. He's happy.

Beat.

URSULA. He doesn't seem happy.

CONNIE. It's a fantastic school. The pastoral care's excellent. That's why we sent him.

Beat.

URSULA. They call him names and hit him. These boys apparently –

CONNIE. They're here. Downstairs. You'll have to go. (*Beat.*) You shouldn't come back. I don't want you coming back here. Okay? (*Beat.*) I don't want to see you again.

URSULA. What about meeting up?

CONNIE. It's best like this.

CONNIE *goes to her bag. She gets out a wad of notes and hands it over to* URSULA, *her hand is shaking.*

URSULA. No.

CONNIE. Take it.

Beat.

URSULA. I don't want it.

Beat. CONNIE *keeps her hand outstretched waiting for* URSULA *to change her mind. After a few moments she stuffs the money back in her bag.*

Beat.

Connie. Are you alright? Do you need –

CONNIE. I don't... need anything. I just need you to leave. (*Beat.*) Please.

Silence.

Ursula.

Silence.

Ursula.

Silence. CONNIE *is becoming more desperate.*

Ursula!

FOUR

2001. A hospital corridor. URSULA *waits.* CONNIE *and* ADRIAN *rush over.*

CONNIE. Ursula!

> CONNIE *hugs* URSULA.

God. I'm so sorry.

URSULA. S'alright.

ADRIAN. The car –

CONNIE. That fucking car!

ADRIAN. I think it was the alternator.

CONNIE. You didn't think that, the AA man told you. We waited over an hour. Nearly got a taxi –

URSULA. Take a breath you're alright.

> *Beat.*

CONNIE. Did we miss it?

URSULA. Yeah. I had to –

CONNIE. Fuck.

URSULA. They couldn't wait –

CONNIE. No, no no yeah of course. They can't wait.

URSULA. I tried to get them to hang on but they wouldn't –

CONNIE. No.

> *Beat.*

ADRIAN. Is everything… okay?

URSULA. Everything's fine.

CONNIE. Really?

> URSULA *nods.* ADRIAN *reaches for* CONNIE*'s hand.*

ADRIAN. Thank God.

CONNIE. It's fine? Everything's all... fine?

    URSULA *nods*.

    And... you found out? Did you find out?

URSULA. Yeah.

CONNIE. Oh my God.

    CONNIE *looks to* ADRIAN. *They squeeze hands, looking at* URSULA *expectantly.*

URSULA. You definitely want to –

CONNIE. Yes. Yes –

ADRIAN. We want to know.

    Beat.

URSULA. It's a boy.

    Silence.

CONNIE. A boy.

    URSULA *nods*.

    Adrian, it's a boy.

    ADRIAN *nods*. *They hug each other.*

URSULA. They can't be like... a hundred per cent –

ADRIAN. Why not?

URSULA. Because sometimes what they think is the... penis... isn't actually the penis.

ADRIAN. What else could it be?

URSULA. I don't know. It's very rare anyway they said and usually mistakes happen the other way around. Like... they say it's a girl but then the penis is hiding.

ADRIAN. The penis is *hiding*? Where might it hide?

URSULA. I don't know but it's not hiding anyway. It's there. They were pretty sure.

ADRIAN. But not a hundred per cent?

CONNIE. Oh, Adrian, stop it.

ADRIAN. Sorry. I'm excited.

> CONNIE *grins*. URSULA *pulls a row of scan photos from her bag and hands them to* CONNIE. *She shows* ADRIAN *and they sit staring*.

CONNIE. He's a boy. Adrian, look there's his little legs. And arms, look! Tiny little arms. Oh my *God*.

> CONNIE *and* ADRIAN *are both lost in the scan photo*. URSULA *sits awkwardly*.

ADRIAN. And there were no other... issues.

URSULA. Nope.

ADRIAN. Health-wise. Everything was...

URSULA. Everything's fine.

CONNIE. He's *perfect*.

ADRIAN. And the size is... normal.

URSULA. Normal size. He's very normal. Average.

CONNIE. Average is great! What a brilliant word. *Average*.

ADRIAN. You've been looking after yourself?

URSULA. Yes.

ADRIAN. Eating off the list?

URSULA. I draw the line at asparagus. Makes me piss reek.

ADRIAN. Everything else though?

URSULA. Trying –

CONNIE. Look at her, she looks great. You look *great*, Urse.

URSULA. Do I?

CONNIE. You've put weight on.

URSULA. I'm pregnant.

CONNIE. On your face. You look like / you're... glowing.

URSULA. I've been sweating a lot. All that garlic comes out through me pores. I get self-conscious.

CONNIE. You don't smell of garlic.

ADRIAN. Is there… anyone I could talk to? Sonographer or a… consultant.

CONNIE. What about?

ADRIAN. The baby.

CONNIE. The baby's fine.

ADRIAN. Yes I just… y'know, peace of mind.

CONNIE. Ursula's told you.

ADRIAN. I appreciate that but –

CONNIE. He's *fine*.

Silence.

ADRIAN. Would anyone like a coffee or a… herbal… tea?

CONNIE. I'd love a coffee, thanks.

ADRIAN. Ursula. Hot drink? Water?

URSULA. I'm alright. I've just had some coke. (*Beat. Off* ADRIAN.) *Coca-Cola.*

Beat.

ADRIAN. Coke's not on the –

CONNIE. Adrian.

Beat.

ADRIAN. I'll be back in a minute then.

CONNIE. Take your time.

ADRIAN leaves. CONNIE smiles at URSULA, rolling her eyes.

Sorry. He gets a bit stressed. (*Beat.*) How are / are *you* okay?

URSULA *nods.*

We had an idea actually / *I* had an idea but Adrian thinks… he thinks it's totally the right thing as well… if *you* think / if… you're up for it. (*Beat.*) That you could live with us for the next few months. (*Beat.*) If you wanted to.

Beat.

URSULA. Connie, I can't do it.

CONNIE. No. Okay. I understand. I wasn't trying to / I just thought it might be easier for you. We could look after –

URSULA. I don't think I can give him up (*Beat*.) The baby. I think / I want to keep him.

Silence.

Connie?

Beat.

CONNIE. I can understand. Seeing it… *him*… just now. Finding out. I get it. That's completely normal / you'd be / if you didn't feel like that it'd be strange… wouldn't it?

Beat.

URSULA. I've felt like this for a while. I've wanted to say for a while.

CONNIE. Why didn't you?

URSULA. I tried. I find it really hard. Talking to you.

CONNIE. Right. That's / okay…

Silence.

How… how would that work then?

URSULA. How would what work?

CONNIE. You. And a baby.

URSULA. I don't know. (*Beat*.) I'd just love him.

CONNIE. You'd just love him.

URSULA. Yeah.

Beat.

CONNIE. With what? What else would you / how would you… do this… exactly?

URSULA. Don't get / don't be angry –

CONNIE. I'm not / I'm not getting angry. I'm listening. I'm waiting. To hear you / what you've got say. (*Beat*.)

I'm confused to be honest, Ursula. I'm feeling very fucking / and scared. Actually.

URSULA. So am I.

CONNIE. Then tell me, talk to me. You're not saying anything. Not really. How, how, how would it... how can you see it working? You and this baby you said you didn't want.

URSULA. It's not perfect.

CONNIE. It's not perfect? That's... hilarious, Ursula. (*Beat.*) What if you get sent down? What happens to him then?

Beat.

URSULA. I've been looking into it.

CONNIE. Looking into it?

URSULA. There's ways I can make it work. Amy said –

CONNIE. I thought she might have something to say –

URSULA. That's what she's there for –

CONNIE. To mess with your head?

URSULA. To support me. It's her job. She said there's ways of keeping us together, me and the baby –

CONNIE. In prison.

URSULA. It happens. I've spoke to other people. I've read stuff –

CONNIE. But you don't *want* him. You told me. Over and over. You don't want him. You won't *love* him.

URSULA. I will.

CONNIE. You don't even know *how* to love someone properly, Ursula –

URSULA. Don't say that. I do. I love you.

CONNIE. You love *me*?

URSULA. Course I love you.

CONNIE. Have I been *hallucinating* for the past twenty years? Was that all a fucking... dream, a *nightmare*?

URSULA. I love you. Do you not love me?

Silence.

CONNIE. It'll be a matter of time. You know that, don't you? Before you go inside again, fall off the wagon, start taking all that... shit again. What's gonna happen then? What is going to happen next time?

URSULA. There won't be a next time.

CONNIE. That's what you said last time. And the time before. (*Pause.*) They'll be on you. Take him off you. Like *that*.

URSULA. He'll give me a reason. He *has* given me a reason. I'm clean. I haven't touched anything for months.

CONNIE. You're a liar.

URSULA. I'm not it's true. It is. You said it yourself, I'm doing alright... I look well.

CONNIE. You look a fucking *mess*.

URSULA. This time. I swear. It's *different*.

CONNIE. This time... always fucking this time. It doesn't work like that, Ursula. Does it? We've been here before. We're *always* here. In this / It's a fucking... cycle. Over and over. You've had your chances, you've fucking had your chances. Give *me* a chance.

URSULA. People change. They do change. Are you saying you don't think I can change?

Beat.

CONNIE. *Yes*. (*Beat.*) Yes I am. That's *exactly* what I'm saying. Eight years. Eight fucking years I've waited for this, don't do it to me please I'm begging you. Don't do it to me. Don't change your mind. You came to *me*. You left it too late, all this fucking time without seeing a doctor. With your head in the sand. (*Beat.*) The one thing I want more than anything in the fucking world and you're taking that away? Five miscarriages, eight rounds of IVF... can you even remember? Or were you too fucked to notice? After everything I've done for you. After *everything*? You said you couldn't do it. You didn't *want* it. You said it, Ursula... it was *you*... 'I don't want a kid, Connie... I don't want it. Please help me, Connie.' Calling it a fucking parasite. (*Beat*.) I'll get on my hands and knees I swear I will. I'm begging you. I'll do anything. Don't do this to me, Ursula.

CONNIE *bends down in front of* URSULA.

URSULA. Stop it.

CONNIE. I am begging.

URSULA. You said 'talk to me'.

CONNIE. Yes. I said 'talk to me'. I didn't say turn around at any point you like and break my fucking heart.

URSULA. Get up. Please. Get up.

CONNIE *gets to her feet, composes herself. She leans against the wall.*

Silence.

What if we did it together?

CONNIE....

URSULA. Me, you, and the baby. (*Beat*.) We could do it together.

Beat.

CONNIE. Are you serious? (*Beat*.) What about *Adrian*?

URSULA. I want to do the right thing. I want my son to be happy.

CONNIE. Your son? Please don't –

URSULA. That's all I want.

CONNIE. He *will* be happy. With us. He needs stability. *Security.*

URSULA. Security. I know.

CONNIE. Adrian is / he'll be a good / he's going to be a brilliant dad. You should see him with his brother's kids (*Beat*.) We're happy. I love him. (*Beat*.) And I love you. I do love you.

URSULA. Do you?

CONNIE. Yes. I do. I *love* you. I love you and I think you're really brave. (*Beat.*) I think you're really brave. And I know how hard this is, how hard it *must* be and how you *think* it'll be different but *you know*... you *know* what the right thing is. You *know* it, Ursula.

Beat.

URSULA. Don't do that.

CONNIE. Do what?

URSULA. Talk to me like that. Like I'm an idiot.

CONNIE. I'm not. I'm not. I'm sorry. Ursula, please. You'll still see him. You will. You can see him... whenever you want. You can. We'd never stop you. And you'll know... you'll *always* know he's *safe*. He's being looked after, that he's going to have a good life –

URSULA. You think I'm scum. (*Beat.*) Don't you?

CONNIE. No –

URSULA. You do. Maybe you haven't admitted it to yourself but you do. You think I'm scum –

CONNIE. Ursula –

URSULA. You think. Same start, same shit to deal with. But look at me and look at *her*... she's a fucking write-off.

CONNIE. No.

URSULA. If you want this baby. If you want him. Tell the *truth*.

CONNIE. I'm telling you the truth.

URSULA. You think I'm a waste of space and you've written me off. You wrote me off a long time ago.

CONNIE. I have *not* written you off.

URSULA. If you want this baby. Just tell me the truth. You said you'd do anything. (*Beat.*) Say you think I'm scum.

CONNIE. Stop it. Please.

Beat.

URSULA. If you want him, say –

CONNIE. I won't say it.

> URSULA *stands to leave*.

> Ursula.

URSULA. Just say it. It's really fucking easy.

> *Silence*.

> Okay. Bye.

> URSULA *starts to walk away.* CONNIE *calls after her.*

CONNIE. I think you're fucking *scum*.

> URSULA *stops. She walks back slowly and sits back down.*

URSULA. Thank you.

> CONNIE *starts to cry*.

> *Silence*.

> ADRIAN *appears, carrying two coffees*.

ADRIAN. Machine was bloody miles away.

> ADRIAN *hands a cup to* CONNIE.

> Everything alright?

> *Beat*.

URSULA. Everything's fine. Everything's great.

> ADRIAN *looks to* CONNIE. *She nods*.

CONNIE. Fine.

> *Beat*.

URSULA. I should go now, though.

ADRIAN. We can give you a lift.

URSULA. I'm alright thanks.

ADRIAN. No we'll take –

URSULA. Car sick. Don't want me retching all over your leather seats, do you?

> *Beat*.

ADRIAN. Really. I don't –

URSULA. I'd rather get the train.

ADRIAN. If you're sure?

URSULA. I'm sure.

ADRIAN. See you next week then?

URSULA. Yeah. See you next week.

> ADRIAN *pulls a wad of notes from his pocket and hands them to* URSULA.

ADRIAN. That's just for / just in case you need… extra.

> *Beat.* URSULA *hesitates before taking the money. She shoves it into her pocket.*
>
> *Silence.*
>
> Okay… well… we'll walk you out / shall we? Shall we walk you out?
>
> URSULA *picks up her bag and walks off ahead.* ADRIAN *follows.*
>
> CONNIE *stays put, clutching the scan photos. She stands watching them go.*

FIVE

1990. Darkness. A cacophony of noise, loud music blaring out.

A light switch is flicked on. CONNIE *stands watching unnoticed by* URSULA *who jumps about, dancing manically.*

This goes on for a while before CONNIE *switches the music off.*

URSULA *stops. Her face lights up when she sees* CONNIE. *She goes to her and wraps her arms around her tightly before taking* CONNIE*'s face in her hands.*

URSULA. You never said you were coming. Why didn't you say?

CONNIE. Who were those people?

URSULA. If I'd have known –

CONNIE. Ursula. (*Beat.*) Who were those *men*?

URSULA. Horrible fuckers. Can I get you anything? You should ring next time. Let me know you're coming. Got me off guard, wasn't expecting you.

CONNIE. This is my flat –

URSULA. Would've tidied up.

CONNIE *pulls a piece of paper from her pocket.*

CONNIE. There's a note from the flat upstairs. Threatening to report me, have me thrown out –

URSULA. Cunts.

CONNIE. How did you get in?

URSULA. Teleported how d'you fuckin' think? Used me key, didn't I?

CONNIE. You haven't *got* a key. I took the key off you, Ursula. I said, didn't I? You can't just turn up any more not like this, not in this state. There's piss in the porch. Someone's pissed there.

URSULA. Fucking dirty bastards.

CONNIE. You're gonna have to clean it up.

CONNIE *starts to move around the room tidying up.*

I said you could stay here then you let me down, then I said you could stay and it happened again, then I said you could stay and it happened again and I can't do this any more now. Honestly, I can't... someone's coming, Ursula. I've got... someone coming and it fucking... *stinks* in here.

URSULA. It's them fuckers. I can't get your windows open, there's some sort of security thing on them.

CONNIE. Who were they?

CONNIE *opens a window.*

URSULA. Pigs.

CONNIE *continues tidying.* URSULA *picks up a can and takes a swig.*

CONNIE. I'm supposed to be making tea for us.

CONNIE *gets on her hands and knees, picking up stuff from the floor. She finds a small plastic bag with white powder inside and tucks it into her pocket.* URSULA *doesn't notice.*

URSULA. I'm not hungry don't worry.

CONNIE. Not for *you*. I'm making tea for someone else.

URSULA. Who?

Beat.

CONNIE. A friend.

URSULA *sits on the arm of the couch. She finishes the can and drops it onto the floor.*

CONNIE *stops. Beat. She picks up the can.* URSULA *looks down at her from above.*

URSULA. Thank you.

URSULA *turns the music back on. She is lost in her own world while* CONNIE *continues to sort out the mess.* CONNIE *switches the music off again.*

After a few moments there's a knock at the door. CONNIE *stops, bracing herself. Another knock.*

Fuck's that? (*Beat*.) If it's those pigs again, Con, tell them you're calling the police.

Beat. CONNIE *opens the door.* ADRIAN *stands there, a bottle of wine in one hand. He leans to kiss* CONNIE.

ADRIAN. Hello.

CONNIE. Hi.

CONNIE *stays at the door, delaying the inevitable.*

ADRIAN. I'm a bit early. Sorry. I was going to wait outside but then I thought / I don't know / you might look out of the window and see me / is everything… are you okay? Can I… come in?

Beat.

CONNIE. Ursula's here.

ADRIAN. Okay –

CONNIE. I didn't / She's in a bit of a… we should probably eat out.

ADRIAN. Well, I should meet her first? Can I? (*Beat. Off* CONNIE.) It's okay.

Resigned, CONNIE *steps out of the way.* ADRIAN *enters and approaches* URSULA.

Hello.

CONNIE. Ursula, this is Adrian.

ADRIAN. Good to meet you, Ursula.

ADRIAN *puts his hand out.* URSULA *looks at it with disdain.*

URSULA. It's a different pig. (*Beat*.) Alright.

Beat.

ADRIAN. I've heard lots about you.

URSULA. Funny that, Adrian, coz I've heard *jack-fucking-shit* about you.

Beat.

CONNIE. Ursula –

URSULA. Sorry, Adrian. (*Beat, to* CONNIE.) Don't want him to think I'm rude, that's all. Him knowing everything about me and I haven't got a fuckin' clue –

CONNIE. He doesn't know everything –

ADRIAN. Connie told me how close you two were.

URSULA. *Were* –

ADRIAN. *Are.*

URSULA. Yeah. We *are.*

ADRIAN. Growing up together.

URSULA. Where *you* from then, Adrian?

ADRIAN. Hampshire. Originally. I moved up here for university and… stayed.

URSULA. Fuck d'you do that for, Adrian? Sorry I'm aware that I keep saying your name but I don't think I've ever met anyone called Adrian before.

Silence.

CONNIE. I met… Adrian… at work.

URSULA. Done well for yourself with your job, haven't you, Con?

ADRIAN. She has. She's very talented –

URSULA. You the boss?

ADRIAN. Well, not –

CONNIE. One of them –

URSULA. That helps –

CONNIE. Not mine. Not directly. We're in different –

URSULA. That allowed then, is it? (*Beat. Off* ADRIAN.) You two.

Beat.

ADRIAN. Yes. Lots of people… meet at work –

CONNIE. And it's early days.

ADRIAN. Yes.

URSULA. It's not an *abuse of power* then.

CONNIE. He's not *my* boss, Ursula.

URSULA. Coz I know all about that –

ADRIAN. We met at a company drinks do.

URSULA. *Company drinks do.* Fuckin' get you. (*Beat.*) How long's it been then?

   Beat.

ADRIAN. Few –

CONNIE. Weeks.

URSULA. She never said that's all, Adrian. Usually tells me everything.

   Beat.

CONNIE. It's been tricky recently.

URSULA. It has been tricky.

CONNIE. Ursula, we're going out.

ADRIAN. Why go out? I'm here now. We could still –

CONNIE. Oh no –

ADRIAN. I'd like to.

CONNIE. Honestly. That's / but I don't think it's a good –

ADRIAN. I'll cook. For… the three of us.

URSULA. That'd be top, that, *Adrian*.

CONNIE. I honestly don't think –

ADRIAN. I *want* to.

URSULA. He wants to.

ADRIAN. Or… I can chat to Ursula if you'd prefer to cook?

CONNIE. No. No… okay. Okay. You make it then… if you're sure / that'd be… really… nice. It's nothing fancy. Spaghetti Bolognese. Everything's there.

ADRIAN. Great.

CONNIE. Only if you're sure?

URSULA. He's sticking some mince in a pan, he's not giving you one of his fuckin' kidneys.

ADRIAN. I'm sure. (*Gestures to kitchen.*) I'll get started.

CONNIE. Yeah. Okay. (*Holding the letter from the neighbour.*) I just need to... deal with something. I won't be a minute.

ADRIAN. It's fine, I'll be fine.

ADRIAN goes into the kitchen.

CONNIE (*to* URSULA). I'm going upstairs. I'll be back in one minute. Just don't / please don't –

URSULA. Don't fucking what?

Beat. CONNIE *leaves. Pause.* URSULA *shouts through to the kitchen.*

Do you think we're alike?

Beat. ADRIAN *appears.*

ADRIAN. Sorry?

URSULA. Me and Connie. Think we're alike?

Beat.

ADRIAN. Yes. (*Beat.*) There's a definite... resemblance.

URSULA. Dunno who we take after. There's a photo of our mum knocking about somewhere but you can't really see her face properly. In my head we look like her but then things tend to be quite different in my head, Adrian, that's part of the problem. It's nice if you can treat her nice. Pay for things. Connie not our mum, I think she's dead. (*Gestures to a can on the floor.*) Could you pass me a drink please, Adrian?

Beat.

ADRIAN. Are you... sure that's a good idea?

URSULA. I'm absolutely positive.

Beat. ADRIAN *passes a can to* URSULA.

You got brothers or sisters?

ADRIAN. A brother.

URSULA. How old?

ADRIAN. Thirty-ish. Early thirties.

URSULA. Don't you know how old your brother is?

ADRIAN. He's thirty-one.

URSULA. You close?

ADRIAN. Not very.

URSULA. That's sad.

ADRIAN. It's fine. We get on. We're just not –

URSULA. Some people aren't. We are. Me and Con. She looks after me. We look after each other. Always have. Bought a card for her birthday, says on the front 'I smile because I'm your sister' and then you open it and on the inside it goes 'I laugh because there's nothing you can do about it.' (*Beat.*) I wrote me own thing as well. I wrote 'You can't pick your family but if you could I'd still pick you.' (*Beat.*) It wasn't exactly me own thing coz I'd seen it on another card. But it is true. I'd pick her if I could. (*Beat.*) If you try to fuck me I'm gonna have to say no because I'm a very very very loyal person.

ADRIAN....

URSULA. I'm joking. I've got a very dry sense of humour. Bit dark. You look like you could be a doctor have you ever thought about it?

ADRIAN. No.

URSULA. Bet you've got a lovely bedside manner.

CONNIE *returns*.

CONNIE. Okay. Everything alright? You okay?

ADRIAN. Yes. No we've just been chatting.

URSULA. He tried to fuck me but I said no because he pissed in our porch.

CONNIE (*to* ADRIAN). I'm not sure this is a good idea –

ADRIAN. It's alright.

URSULA. I said I'd never do that to you. Ever. Can't blame him though he's only human.

CONNIE. Just ignore her.

URSULA. Just ignore me, Adrian.

Beat.

ADRIAN. I'll carry on.

CONNIE. I'll... show you where everything is.

ADRIAN and CONNIE leave. URSULA checks they've gone then sits up, reaching into her pockets and looking for something. She scans the room then gets down on her hands and knees onto the floor scrabbling around.

URSULA (*shouting*). Connie? Where'd you put everything? When you were cleaning up?

Beat. CONNIE appears.

CONNIE. In the bin.

Beat.

URSULA. Me stuff. Did you find it? Where'd you put it?

CONNIE. Chucked it.

URSULA. Connie, fuck off now –

CONNIE. Lower your voice and calm down. I told you last time.

URSULA. Give it me back.

CONNIE. It's gone.

URSULA. No.

CONNIE. It's gone. It's in the bin.

URSULA rushes to look.

The bin outside.

URSULA rushes to the door, CONNIE blocks her path.

You promised me.

URSULA. Out the fuckin' way, Con.

ADRIAN *appears in an apron holding a kitchen knife.*

ADRIAN. Okay hey let's just calm everything down –

URSULA (*shouting*). Fuck off! Who the fuck are you? (*Beat. To* CONNIE.) Who the fuck is he?

CONNIE. I said you couldn't come here like this again. I told you. I keep telling you.

URSULA. Tell him to go.

CONNIE. No.

URSULA. Tell him to fucking get out.

CONNIE. No. (*Beat.*) I want him to stay.

URSULA. You don't even fucking *know* him.

CONNIE. I do know him. This is my flat and I want him here. (*Beat, to* ADRIAN.) Jesus, I'm so sorry.

URSULA. We're alright. We've always been alright –

CONNIE. We're not alright –

URSULA. And now you're fucking being like *this*?

ADRIAN. Look everything's okay. Let's just –

URSULA. Shut. The. Fuck. Up. Nobody is talking to you. Connie, let me out.

URSULA *charges at the door,* CONNIE *pushes her back.* ADRIAN *intervenes, he puts the knife down out of the way and tries to hold* URSULA. URSULA *lashes out and punches him.* CONNIE *recoils.*

ADRIAN (*holding his face*). It's alright. I'm okay.

URSULA *grabs the knife and pulls up her sleeve.*

CONNIE. Stop it, Ursula. Put it down.

URSULA *runs the blade across her own arm, drawing blood.*

URSULA. Open the door.

CONNIE. Stop it.

ADRIAN *grabs the knife and holds it up high. He opens the door for* URSULA *and she runs out.* CONNIE *bursts into tears and he puts his arms around her.*

ADRIAN. It's okay. Come on.

CONNIE. I didn't want you to see this.

ADRIAN. It's okay. Come on. It doesn't matter.

CONNIE. Of course it *matters* –

ADRIAN. To *me*. Nothing's changed. (*Beat.*) I don't want you to hide anything from me... I *never* want you to hide anything from me.

CONNIE *nods.*

CONNIE. I don't know what to do. I'm so / fucking desperately /

ADRIAN. You don't have to do it on your own. (*Beat.*) I'm not going anywhere okay? I promise. I love you. (*Pause.*) Sorry that's not... ideal. Right now. The timing... But I do. (*Beat.*) I love you. I want to look after you... keep you safe.

Silence. CONNIE *and* ADRIAN *stand, arms around each other.*

URSULA *enters carrying a large bin bag. She drags it to the middle of the floor and tips it out before scrabbling around in the contents.*

CONNIE *watches her do this for a few moments before pulling a small clear plastic bag out of her pocket.*

CONNIE *drops the bag at* URSULA's *feet then walks out followed by* ADRIAN.

SIX

1985. CONNIE*'s flat, small and bare apart from a couple of pieces of furniture. On a side table is a pint glass with a small bunch of flowers in.*

URSULA *stands, looking around. There's a bin bag at her feet.* CONNIE *is trying to gauge her reaction.*

CONNIE. What d'you reckon?

URSULA. Yeah.

CONNIE. Better than the old one?

URSULA. I liked the old one.

CONNIE. View's good. You can see the park.

> URSULA *goes to the window and looks out silently for a while before turning her attention back to the room.*

Bought you flowers.

> CONNIE *points to the glass.* URSULA *nods.*

URSULA. We should hang pictures.

CONNIE. Yeah.

URSULA. Make it more homely. Put photos up. You still got some?

CONNIE. Yeah. Must have. Somewhere.

URSULA. Norma's got a whole wall. All the kids she's ever had. Put me on it.

CONNIE. Did she?

URSULA. Only been there three months. Put us in a frame and everything. Next to *Melissa.* Melissa's been there for years. Norma said there's no difference in her eyes.

Beat.

CONNIE. Been alright there then, has it? At Norma's.

URSULA. Yeah. (*Beat.*) She got me this.

> URSULA *thrusts her hand forward to show* CONNIE *a watch she's wearing.*

Present for going. Sort of like a joke coz I'm always late aren't I? She goes 'I don't want you forgetting the time when you come back and see us.' (*Beat*.) She was sad, y'know?

CONNIE. Was she?

URSULA. She goes 'I don't get like this about everyone, Ursula.'

CONNIE. Thought you're all the same?

URSULA. She says that but you know what some of them are like. Told you about Carl, didn't I? Lad before me. Did a shit on the stairs and set fire to his duvet.

CONNIE. Is he on the wall?

URSULA. Not any more.

Beat.

CONNIE. Reckon you will, then? (*Beat*.) Go back and see her?

URSULA. Yeah. She said anytime, like.

CONNIE. Did she?

URSULA. Every kid's family Norma said.

CONNIE. Apart from Carl.

URSULA. Yeah coz he were a fucking nutcase. (*Beat*.) She's got this little picture on the wall by the door as you come in… *tapestry*. It says 'Blood makes you related, love makes you family.'

Beat.

CONNIE. People say things, Ursula. They make promises and they can't always keep them, you know that.

URSULA. She didn't promise anything she just said to go back and see her –

CONNIE. I know but even that… telling you to go round, buying you things. Making you feel like that.

URSULA. Like what?

CONNIE. Special.

Silence.

Doesn't mean she doesn't *care* but you can't take it too serious. It's her job innit? End of the day.

URSULA *nods. Silence*.

Sorry I haven't been getting over as much lately.

URSULA. It's alright.

CONNIE. Been a bit mad with college. Two hours door to door an' that. Fare and everything too.

URSULA. Yeah yeah. I know.

CONNIE. Didn't want you thinking anything. Didn't care or something. Not that you would. Just been mental. And hey I got a job... did I tell you I got a job? *Hairdresser's*. Washing hair. Cash in hand. Just Saturdays. And every other Sunday.

Beat.

URSULA. Hardly gonna see you.

CONNIE. Course you will, what you talkin' about?

URSULA. Sat on me own.

CONNIE. Trying to get some money. Gotta do that, haven't I? Look after us.

Beat. URSULA *nods*.

Should think about school too. There's one round the corner.

URSULA. No.

CONNIE. Norma said you've been good lately, going in.

URSULA. Not fucking starting another one. Going through all that again.

CONNIE. What you gonna do all day?

URSULA. Stay here. Wait for you. (*Beat*.) Is there a telly?

CONNIE. Not yet.

Silence.

URSULA. I got some forms.

CONNIE. What forms?

URSULA. Norma give us them.

> URSULA *bends down and unties the bin bag tipping the contents – a heap of clothing and various possessions into a heap – out onto the floor. She finds a crumpled piece of paper and hands it to* CONNIE.

> Child benefit.

> CONNIE *takes the form and stares at it.* URSULA *continues to look through the bin bag, she finds another form and hands that to* CONNIE *too.*

> Have to do this one first though Norma says or you won't get nothing.

> CONNIE *scans the forms.* URSULA *peers over her shoulder.*

> *Legal…* what's that?

CONNIE. *Guardianship.*

URSULA. You gonna be me mum now?

CONNIE. How the fuck can I be your *mum*?

> *Beat.*

URSULA. Have to do them soon as. Norma said to tell you.

CONNIE (*reading*). Doesn't even make *sense*. I can't even… what do I do with this?

URSULA. She said you can call her if you're stuck.

CONNIE. I'm not stuck.

> *Silence.*

> CONNIE *stares at the form.*

URSULA. Con? (*Beat.*) I'm starving.

> CONNIE *folds both the forms and tucks them away.*

CONNIE. Right. Yeah. (*Beat.*) I was gonna go the chippy for us. Fancy the chippy?

URSULA. Yeah.

CONNIE *grabs her coat. She pulls out a small handful of coins and then roots through her other pockets.*

CONNIE. Shit, I don't think / I haven't got... hang on.

She counts out a small pile and puts it to one side.

That's for the meter.

URSULA *reaches into her pocket and holds a note out to* CONNIE.

Where d'you get that from?

URSULA. Norma give it us.

Beat.

CONNIE. Keep it. I'll make us something else. Get me money tomorrow, I'll take us then.

URSULA. Don't be a dickhead.

CONNIE. Probably shut now anyway. What time is it?

URSULA (*looking at her watch*). Nine o'clock.

CONNIE. Yeah. They'll be shut.

URSULA. Sort of chippy shuts at nine?

CONNIE. That one.

URSULA. Norma does her own. Got one of them deep-fat fryers.

CONNIE. I'll do us beans on toast.

Pause. CONNIE *walks off to the kitchen.*

URSULA *sits. She puts her head in her hands. A couple of seconds later* CONNIE *shouts through to her.*

(*Off.*) We haven't got any beans.

CONNIE *comes back in.*

Can you just have toast?

CONNIE *stops.* URSULA *looks up, rubbing her eyes.*

Beat.

What's up?

URSULA. Nothin'.

CONNIE *goes and sits next to* URSULA.

CONNIE. Tell us.

URSULA *shakes her head. Beat.*

I'll make it nice. I promise.

URSULA. Isn't the flat. (*Beat.*) Just got a weird… feelin'.

CONNIE. What like?

URSULA *shrugs. Beat.*

URSULA. In me belly. In me head. (*Beat.*) All that.

Beat.

CONNIE. Yeah.

Silence.

I've missed you so much, Urse.

Silence.

You missed me?

URSULA. Yeah. Course I have.

Silence. CONNIE *puts her arms around* URSULA *then, glancing down, notices something. Beat.* CONNIE *takes hold of* URSULA's *wrist,* URSULA *pulls her sleeve down.* CONNIE *pushes it back up to reveal fresh cut marks.*

Silence.

CONNIE. Thought you'd stopped all that.

URSULA *yanks her arm back and pulls her sleeve down, moving away from* CONNIE.

URSULA. I have. Got meself in a state, didn't I?

CONNIE. About what?

URSULA. Dunno. Just got worked up.

CONNIE. Why d'you get worked up?

URSULA. Just did. You know I get worked up.

Pause.

CONNIE. Gotta fuckin' stop it, Ursula.

URSULA. I have.

CONNIE. Pack it in.

URSULA. I will.

CONNIE. Swear.

URSULA. I swear.

Silence.

CONNIE. When you seeing Mandy next?

URSULA. It's not Mandy no more. It's a man called Owen. I'm not keen.

CONNIE. Why not?

URSULA (*shrugging*). Just not. Seeing him Thursday (*Beat.*) You're supposed to come.

CONNIE. Am I?

URSULA (*nodding*). Supposed to be there, meet him.

CONNIE. Why?

URSULA. Dunno. Coz. (*Beat.*) You're me person, aren't you?

Beat.

CONNIE. Got college Thursday. (*Pause.*) But that's alright. (*Beat.*) I'll come.

URSULA. He reeks of TCP.

Silence.

CONNIE. Feels empty now but I'll make it alright. (*Beat.*) Get a telly. (*Beat.*) Do a photo wall.

URSULA. Can I put one up of me and her?

CONNIE....

URSULA. Photo. Got one of me and Norma.

URSULA pulls away from CONNIE to look through the bin bag. She finds a small photo in a frame and hands it to CONNIE.

Can I put it on the wall?

Beat.

CONNIE. If you want. Yeah.

Pause.

URSULA. Can I have me toast now?

CONNIE. Fuck. Sorry, yeah.

CONNIE goes into the kitchen. URSULA looks at the photo. A few moments later and CONNIE returns with toast on a plate. She hands it to URSULA then sits back down, watching URSULA anxiously as she eats.

URSULA. You not having any?

CONNIE. Not hungry. I've emptied a drawer for you. In the bedroom. Middle one.

URSULA nods.

I'll put your stuff in it for you if you want?

URSULA. Yeah alright.

Beat. CONNIE gets on her hands and knees and starts to pile all of URSULA's belongings back into the bin bag.

URSULA stands still eating her toast. She leaves her plate and walks out of the room.

CONNIE watches her go.

SEVEN

1983. CONNIE *runs on breathless, she stops hands on hips, catching her breath and looking around.*

CONNIE (*shouting*). It's tig not hide and seek, you bastard cheat!

She moves around the space, searching, suppressing a giggle.

Stop it now! Come on!

Silence. She waits.

Right, I'm goin'... see ya.

Silence.

When I get in I'm gonna give Cheryl massive tits and a tash.

Suddenly URSULA *appears behind* CONNIE, *running at speed she jumps on her back.*

URSULA. Tig!

CONNIE *screams the two of them fall to the floor laughing.* URSULA *pins* CONNIE's *arms to the ground as she straddles her.*

Touch me Buck's Fizz poster and you're fuckin' dead.

CONNIE (*still laughing*). Get off me!

They wrestle on the floor for a bit, screaming with laughter before CONNIE *yelps with pain. She sits up rubbing her arm.* URSULA *stays lying on the ground.*

Fuckin' hurt me then... go too far you do.

URSULA. Shurrup.

CONNIE. Wanker. It'll be bruised that.

URSULA. Soz.

CONNIE. Always starts out as a laugh then you have to fuckin' push it, don't you?

URSULA. Said sorry.

Silence.

Want me to sing for you?

CONNIE. No I don't. I'm going back now.

URSULA. Ah c'mon –

CONNIE. No… you've pissed me off.

*Silence. They both stay put. CONNIE facing away from
URSULA.*

*URSULA starts to sing the first verse of 'The Land of Make
Believe' by Bucks Fizz, very gently, in almost a whisper.*

*CONNIE is desperately trying not to smile, she looks away
as URSULA continues singing. By the time she reaches the
end of the verse, CONNIE is laughing.*

*URSULA leaps up to her feet and starts to shout out the
chorus, rather than sing, all for CONNIE's amusement. She
jumps around on the spot holding a pretend mic. When she
finishes the chorus, URSULA leaps up on CONNIE again.*

Fuck off!

*URSULA jumps off and wraps her arms around her instead
in a bear hug. They stand arms around each other for
a moment.*

What you being mental for?

URSULA. Not mental. I'm happy.

CONNIE. Are you?

*URSULA pulls away from CONNIE. She fumbles in her
pocket and brings out a small wrapped box. She hands it
to CONNIE.*

URSULA. Happy birthday.

CONNIE. It's not me birthday.

URSULA. Will be.

CONNIE. In three weeks. Give it us then.

URSULA. Ah c'mon, I'm excited.

Beat. CONNIE *takes the present from* URSULA.

CONNIE. Where'd you get the money for a present?

URSULA. Shut your face and open it.

URSULA *hovers excitedly as* CONNIE *tears off the wrapping paper and opens the box. Inside is a small silver locket.* CONNIE *takes it out and holds it up.*

CONNIE. Urse.

URSULA. D'you like it?

CONNIE. Yeah it's gorgeous.

URSULA. Honest?

CONNIE. Honest.

CONNIE *opens the locket. There's an inscription. She reads.*

'Happy Christmas, Doreen. With love always.'

CONNIE *looks up at* URSULA.

URSULA. Fuck. Sorry. I sort of nicked it.

CONNIE. Where from?

URSULA. The shop.

CONNIE. What fucking shop, Ursula?

URSULA. Argos.

CONNIE. Can't even steal from Argos. How can you steal from Argos? It's just catalogues.

URSULA. I pretended I'd ordered something when I hadn't. They called the number and I stuck me hand up. Lad never even asked to see me ticket. Could've been anythin' really. Set of fuckin'… screwdrivers or somethin'. Made up when I opened it.

CONNIE. That's shithouse that is. Someone's had it engraved.

URSULA. D'you like it though?

CONNIE. Yeah I do. Poor fuckin' Doreen.

URSULA. Some prick in a suit buying. Saw him go up to the lad on the till so I legged it. Afford another one can't he?

CONNIE. What if he caught you?

URSULA. He were a fat bastard. Big red face. Would've had a heart attack if he ran.

URSULA takes the necklace from CONNIE and fastens it around her neck. CONNIE peers down at it.

CONNIE. Thank you though. Won't take it off –

URSULA. Let me come with you.

Pause. A look between them.

CONNIE. Been through this, Urse. Been through it like a million times. They won't let us. Not a fuckin' chance –

URSULA. I don't mean tellin' them… askin' them. I mean just doin' it.

CONNIE. No.

URSULA. Why not?

CONNIE. Coz they'll call the police and they'll just stick you back. Put you somewhere else. Somewhere worse. You can't run away.

URSULA. I'm not running away, I'm going with you.

CONNIE. Urse –

URSULA. If you're an adult –

CONNIE. Sixteen. Not proper –

URSULA. Have sex, live on your own… get *married*… but I can't fuckin' come live with you? S'all wrong that.

CONNIE. Don't make the rules do I?

URSULA. Yeah but –

CONNIE. I don't wanna talk about it no more, Ursula.

Silence. URSULA turns her back on CONNIE.

Still see each other all the time. You can come and stay with me. When I'm eighteen. We'll get a flat –

URSULA. Why you still talkin' about it when you don't wanna talk about it?

Beat.

CONNIE. Get a dog.

URSULA *spins around.*

URSULA. Fuck off. You serious?

CONNIE. Get a pet yeah, why not?

URSULA. You said dog. Don't start saying pet like it's gonna end up being a terrapin, fuckin'… goldfish or somethin'.

CONNIE. We'll get a dog.

URSULA. Can we call it Patch?

CONNIE. If you want.

URSULA *is beaming.*

Just gotta wait. I'll sort things out. Get a job.

URSULA. What job you gonna get?

CONNIE. Dunno yet.

Beat.

URSULA. Know what you could do?

CONNIE. What?

URSULA. Pictures. You could be one of them people who rip the tickets and carry the tray of ice creams.

CONNIE. Could yeah.

URSULA. Let us in for nowt… I'll sit at the back. Watch films all day. Pig in shit. (*Beat.*) Be a brilliant job that. Patch can come too.

CONNIE. No he fuckin' can't. He'll piss on the seats.

URSULA. He won't. I'll train him. Teach him tricks and everything.

Silence.

Where you gonna go, Con?

CONNIE. Dunno yet. Got numbers. Hostels and that.

URSULA. Are you scared?

Beat.

CONNIE. No. Course I'm not.

URSULA. I am. (*Beat.*) What about the nights? Can't hack it in the nights when you're not there. Y'know what I'm like with the dark, what I get like. Won't feel safe. Get meself worked up.

CONNIE. Know what I do… when I get like that?

CONNIE *wraps her arms around herself and starts to chant.*

I love you I love you I love you I love you.

She stops. URSULA *is laughing.*

URSULA. Fuck off! Not doin' that to meself. Not sayin' I fuckin' love meself.

CONNIE. Don't have to say it about yourself. (*Beat.*) I say it about you.

URSULA. Do you?

CONNIE. Yeah.

Pause.

URSULA. I'll do it but I'm saying it about you, yeah? Not saying I fuckin' love meself. And I don't wanna do that… shit… with me arms.

CONNIE. Nah you gotta do that bit. That's the whole point of it. Giving yourself a hug when I'm not there.

URSULA. You're a right freak sometimes you are.

CONNIE *continues.*

CONNIE. I love you I love you I love you I love you…

URSULA *wraps her arms around herself and starts to chant too. They both laugh as they chant.*

CONNIE/URSULA. I love you I love you I love you I love you –

URSULA. Fuckin' hell… this is *mental*.

CONNIE. Shut up… keep doing it.

CONNIE/URSULA. I love you I love you I love you I love you I love you…

Gradually the laughter stops.

I love you I love you I love you I love you.

CONNIE *and* URSULA *wrap their arms around each other, clinging tightly.* CONNIE *starts to prise herself away but* URSULA *holds on silently.*

CONNIE. I love you I love you I love you I love you…

It's a struggle as CONNIE *has to wrench herself away from* URSULA; *it's as though they are being prised apart by some unseen force.*

After a few more moments they are ripped away from each other violently.

CONNIE *is left alone.*

EIGHT

2020. A park. CONNIE *sits on a bench, a melting ice cream in each hand.*

She waits.

After a while URSULA *appears.* CONNIE *stands as she approaches.*

CONNIE. Hello.

URSULA. I'm late. Sorry. I was on a different bench. This makes more sense now. By the playground.

CONNIE. Sorry I did say / didn't I say?

URSULA. No yeah you did. You did. You said. By the playground. The one down there's next to them funny exercise machines. I sat down and I thought this isn't a play– / it's not what you'd call a playground.

Beat.

CONNIE. Thank you for coming. (*Beat.*) I wasn't sure if…

Silence.

Beat. CONNIE *hands over the ice cream to* URSULA.

I had to lick the sides sorry / shall we … d'you want to sit down? We could go somewhere else if you want. Inside. Café or somewhere?

URSULA. This is fine.

They both sit.

(*Pointing.*) There's the playground here's the bench. It's the menopause. It's a thing apparently. Low oestrogen. Addles your brain. I'm forever searching for things. Put something down, that's it.

CONNIE *nods, mouthful of ice cream.*

CONNIE. I have night terrors. Wake up screaming sometimes. Drenched in sweat. They never take you seriously, do they? At the doctor's. Fob you off with evening primrose –

URSULA. I'm sorry / I can't / I've given up sugar.

URSULA *holds her ice cream out.*

CONNIE. Oh right… no yeah. (*She takes the ice cream off* URSULA.) It was a spur-of-the-moment thing I saw the van and I thought –

URSULA. It's supposed to help with the brain fog but I dunno if it's made that much difference. They reckon that after a couple of weeks the craving stops but that's bullshit. Been two months now and I could still rip someone's fuckin' throat out for a Mars Bar.

CONNIE. I'll stick them in the bin. Look. Gone. It's fine.

CONNIE *drops the ice creams into the bin.*

URSULA. Lost a bit of weight so that's something.

CONNIE. You look good.

URSULA. Turned fifty in May.

CONNIE. I know.

Beat.

URSULA. Still feel like a *child…* most of the time. Inside. Like a little kid. Then I see this woman. This fifty-year-old woman. And I think… how the fuck did that happen then?

CONNIE. Where did she come from?

Silence.

I left Adrian.

URSULA. Did you?

CONNIE. A year ago. He cried like a baby and said he was going to kill himself and that he hoped I'd be able to shoulder that burden for the rest of my miserable fucking life. Then he met a woman called Helen. (*Beat.*) They're on a walking holiday in Croatia this week.

CONNIE *starts laughing.* URSULA *is silent.*

Sorry. I don't know why I'm laughing I don't find it in the slightest bit –

URSULA. What d'you want, Connie? (*Beat*.) I don't mean to sound / I'm just not sure what I'm doing here. (*Beat*.) Is he okay? Is he / is Jack alright?

Beat.

CONNIE. Yes. Yes. He's fine... he's really really. (*Beat*.) He's amazing. Actually. (*Pause*.) I told him, Ursula. I told him everything. He knows... everything.

Silence.

URSULA. When?

CONNIE. After / when I left Adrian.

Silence.

URSULA. Did he remember me?

CONNIE. Yes.

Silence.

URSULA. Why?

CONNIE....

URSULA. Why tell him then? (*Beat*.) Why tell him at all?

CONNIE. Because it was the right time. (*Beat*.) Because it's the *truth*. Isn't that enough?

URSULA. What *is* the truth though, Connie? I dunno.

CONNIE. I do.

Silence.

My first memory. Is holding you in my arms.

I've got a cushion on my lap and you're lying across it and I've got my arms around you and you're looking up at me and you must be... days... *hours* old. I don't know. But in my head it's just us. And I've got you.

I *remember*.

Taking your hand and wrapping my fingers around it and holding it and thinking to myself I would *always* hold your hand and I would never let go. It felt like you belonged to me. That we belonged to each other.

And I haven't felt that in quite the same way about anybody since.

That's the truth.

I want you to forgive me, Ursula. I understand if you can't I really do but –

URSULA. Forgive you for what?

Beat.

CONNIE. Everything.

URSULA. There's nothing to forgive.

CONNIE. Oh God there is.

URSULA. I don't / I'm sorry… I shouldn't have come. This isn't… *fucking hell.* I don't need this. It's not mine. It's not fair. This is about *you.* Connie. *Your* shit –

CONNIE. It's about *us.* There's so much to –

URSULA. You're sat there talking about belonging… I don't *belong* to you. Not any more, in fact I never have. I'm sorry if everything's gone to shit.

CONNIE. It hasn't gone to shit –

URSULA. I'm not *part* of you. I don't even really know *you,* Con. Not now… not really. (*Beat.*) Sorry but if it's the truth you want so badly then there it is.

URSULA *goes to walk away.* CONNIE *wipes tears away from her face and stands to go after her.*

CONNIE. No. Ursula. Please – (*Beat.*)

URSULA. I can't / I can't do this.

CONNIE. Please wait.

JACK *appears. He is holding a baby.*

URSULA *stops. They stand in front of one another.* CONNIE *stands back.*

Long silence.

JACK. Hiya.

Silence.

This is Romy.

Beat.

URSULA. This is your / you've got a baby?

JACK *nods. Silence.*

JACK. D'you want to hold her? (*Beat.*) You can if you want.

Beat.

URSULA. I was / Sorry I can't / I was going to go. This is all –

JACK. Could you stay? (*Beat.*) Just for a bit. Please.

Beat. URSULA *nods. She heads back to the bench and*
JACK *follows.* CONNIE *stands and steps away making*
space for them.

URSULA *and* JACK *sit.* JACK *still holding the baby close*
to him and patting her back.

She hates going in her pram… wants to be held all the time.

URSULA *nods.*

They like having their back patted like this 'cause it's like
the mother's heartbeat apparently… like being back inside…
in the womb. Makes them feel safe.

Silence.

Would you / d'you want to hold her?

Beat. URSULA *nods. She looks to* CONNIE *who is standing*
watching intently. JACK *places the baby gently in*
URSULA*'s arms.*

URSULA (*to the baby*). Hello. (*She pats her back and gently*
rocks her.) There… you're safe.

Silence. URSULA *is entranced.*

CONNIE. She's got your eyes.

URSULA. Has she?

CONNIE *nods*.

CONNIE. And your chin.

URSULA. Poor bugger.

Silence. URSULA *still lost in the moment. Some time passes.*

There's such a lot to say, isn't there?

Silence.

JACK *strokes his daughter's head.* URSULA *watches him intently, still gently rocking the baby.*

CONNIE *turns to go.*

(To the baby.) It's okay. *(Patting the baby's back gently.)* There. It's alright. *(Beat.)* It's alright now.

CONNIE *stops and watches from the sidelines.* URSULA *looks up at her. They lock eyes.*

A Nick Hern Book

Run Sister Run first published as a paperback original in Great Britain in 2020 by Nick Hern Books Limited, The Glasshouse, 49a Goldhawk Road, London W12 8QP, in association with Sheffield Theatres, Paines Plough and Soho Theatre

Run Sister Run copyright © 2020 Chloë Moss

Chloë Moss has asserted her right to be identified as the author of this work

Cover image: The Other Richard

Designed and typeset by Nick Hern Books, London
Printed in Great Britain by Mimeo Ltd, Huntingdon, Cambridgeshire PE29 6XX

A CIP catalogue record for this book is available from the British Library

ISBN 978 1 84842 958 1

Amateur Performing Rights Applications for performance, including readings and excerpts, by amateurs in the English language throughout the world should be addressed to the Performing Rights Manager, Nick Hern Books, The Glasshouse, 49a Goldhawk Road, London W12 8QP, *tel* +44 (0)20 8749 4953, *email* rights@nickhernbooks.co.uk, except as follows:

Australia: ORiGiN Theatrical, Level 1, 213 Clarence Street, Sydney NSW 2000, *tel* +61 (2) 8514 5201, *email* enquiries@originmusic.com.au, *web* www.origintheatrical.com.au

New Zealand: Play Bureau, PO Box 9013, St Clair, Dunedin 9047, *tel* (3) 455 9959, *email* info@playbureau.com

USA and Canada: Casarotto Ramsay and Associates Ltd, see details below

Professional Performing Rights Applications for performance by professionals in any medium and in any language throughout the world should be addressed to Casarotto Ramsay and Associates Ltd, *email* rights@casarotto.co.uk, www.casarotto.co.uk

No performance of any kind may be given unless a licence has been obtained. Applications should be made before rehearsals begin. Publication of this play does not necessarily indicate its availability for amateur performance.